Reading Mastery Plus

Workbook C

Level 2

SRA

A Division of The McGraw-Hill Companies

Columbus, Ohio

www.sra4kids.com

SRA/McGraw-Hill

A Division of The McGraw·Hill Companies

Send all inquiries to:
SRA/McGraw-Hill
8787 Orion Place
Columbus, OH 43240-4027

Printed in the United States of America.

ISBN 0-07-569092-6

6 7 8 9 DBH 06 05

Name _____

1. Aunt Mary put her pie near the stool and Wilber sat on it.

2. Uncle Henry talked to little Billy as he shaved.

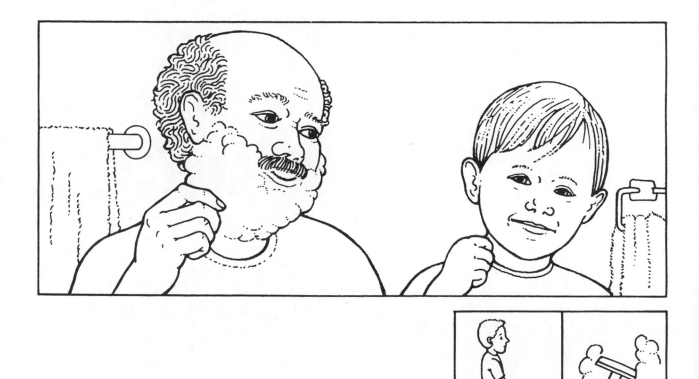

Name _____

Fill in the blanks.

1. Tubby works near _____.

   • Bay Hill   • Bay Town   • Bay Bee

2. Which boat was the fastest? _____

   • Tubby   • Wave Runner   • Red Cat

3. Where did the motorboats and Tubby stay at night?

   _____

   • Dock One   • Dock Two   • Dock Three

4. Which boat at Dock Three was dumpy? _____

5. Which boat at Dock Three was the strongest?

   _____

6. If a big ship ran into the dock, it would

   _____.

   • smash everything   • stop   • fall apart

7. Which boat made a lot of smoke? _____

1. Circle the one who is sitting.
2. Box the one who is sleeping.
3. Make a **C** on the one who is clawing.
4. Make an **m** on the one who will get mad at the cat.

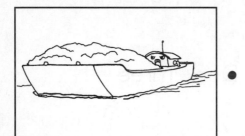

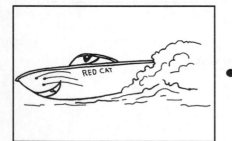

- I am the fastest boat in the bay.

- I push big ships and bar<u>ge</u>s.

- I am fast, but not as fast as Red Cat.

- If I ran into a dock, I would smash everything.

- All the fun boats want to be near me.

- Fun boats say "phew" when they are near me.

Side 2

pig

9

1. Draw a roof on the house.
2. Circle the door.
3. Draw a pig under the word **pig.**
4. Box the thing that is a number.

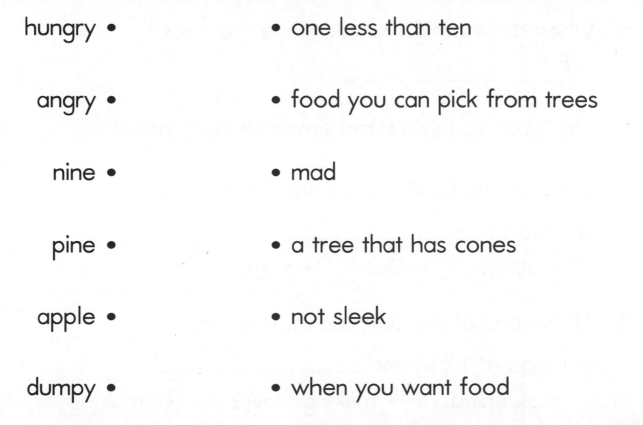

hungry •   • one less than ten

angry •   • food you can pick from trees

nine •   • mad

pine •   • a tree that has cones

apple •   • not sleek

dumpy •   • when you want food

Fill in the blanks.

1. What did Tubby do when she started to work?

   _____

   • honked her horn   • rang a bell   • flashed a light

2. How many times did Tubby honk her horn in the morning?

   _____

3. Tubby also honked her horn when she

   stopped _____.

   • eating   • working   • playing

4. What time did Tubby start work? _____

   • three o'clock   • six o'clock   • noon

5. When did the motorboats leave the dock?

   _____

6. Did Tubby spend a lot of time watching them? _____

7. Some of the boats would ask Tubby if she

   wanted to _____.

   • sleep   • sink   • ra<u>ce</u>

8. At the end of the day, the motorboats

   got mad at Tubby for _____.

   • sleeping   • making waves   • smoking

Side 2

- Honk, honk, honk.

- I wish the wizard was here.

- The wind is blowing me toward Dock Three.

- I will try to scare the monster.

- This is not home. This is Rome.

- I push big boats around the bay.

- Away, away.

1. Write the word **shouting** in the box.
2. Make a line over the first letter.
3. Make a dot under the last letter.
4. Make a box around the letter that is before **u.**
5. Write the word **no** below the big box.

1. At night, what came into the bay?

   _____

   • a fish   • a storm   • a tug boat

2. What did the storm push out of place? _____

   • a ship   • a boat   • a barge

3. The barge was headed for _____.

   • Dock Three   • a ship   • the beach

4. Did the storm wake up the motorboats? _____

5. Did the storm wake up Tubby? _____

6. What did the barge do when it was very close to the dock?

   _____

   • honked two times   • flashed its lights

   • honked three times

7. Did that wake Tubby? _____

8. Who yelled, "Help us"? _____

1. What was going to smash the boats at Dock Three?

   _____

   • a wave   • a ship   • a barge

2. Who went between the barge and the dock?

   _____

3. Did Tubby stop that barge? _____

4. Where did Tubby push the barge?

   _____

   • into the bay   • into the dock   • on the beach

5. Why did Tubby stop out there?

   _____

   • Her motor had blown.   • It was dark.
              • She wanted to play.

6. Who towed Tubby back to the dock? _____

7. Are all the boats pals now? _____

store •   • big

large •   • a place where you buy things

fast •   • not slow

tug •   • not awake

asleep •   • a boat that pushes other boats

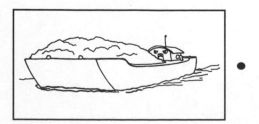

•   • It goes on your hand.

•   • It likes to sit.

•   • It almost rammed into Dock Three.

•   • It has new red paint.

Name _____

1. Rolla was unhappy because she was close to

   _____.

   • a painting　　• horse 8　　• horse 2

2. What did Rolla do to get far from horse 8?

   _____

   • jumped up　　• went faster　　• went slower

3. When Rolla slowed down, what did the other horses do?

   _____

4. What did the music do? _____

5. Some of the other horses _____.

   • went faster　　• laughed at Rolla　　• painted Rolla

6. When Rolla woke up the next morning, she saw

   _____.

   • horse 8　　• the moon and sun

   　　• mountains and valleys

7. Is Rolla happy now? _____

Side 1

- • I am king of all the animals.

- • I am so strong I can move big ships.

- • I can't take the vow of a genie.

- • I want to find out more rules so I can get out of here.

- • I changed a frog into a king.

| love | angry | skates | light | school | picnic |

Name _____

A.

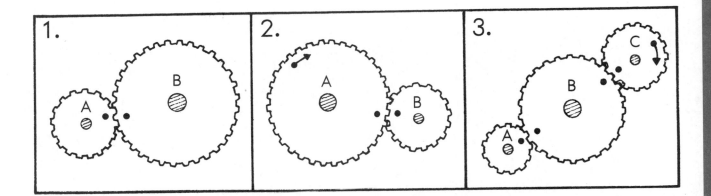

B.

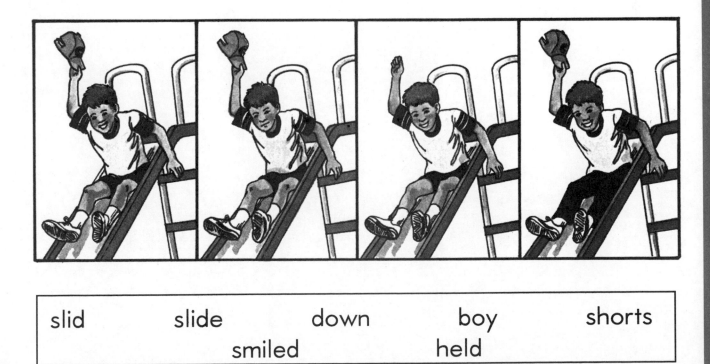

slid	slide	down	boy	shorts
	smiled		held	

Name _____

1. Make a line under each thing that Molly made.

   • phone   • robot   • toaster   • truck

      • racing boat   • pen   • folding chair

2. Did Molly make any things that were perfect? _____

3. What did Molly's toaster do to some of the slices?

   _____

   • burned them   • smashed them   • folded them

4. What was the best thing that Molly made?

   _____

   • a racing boat   • Bleep   • a folding chair

5. How many years did it take Molly to make Bleep?

   _____

6. Who did Bleep sound like? _____

7. Did Bleep always tell the truth? _____

The boy walked home.

1. Make a line under the first two words.

2. Who walked home? _____

3. Box the words that tell who walked home.

4. Where did the boy walk? _____

5. Circle the word that tells where the boy walked.

| lake | red | 8 | sheep | perfect |

1. Help, a big wolf is after the _____.

2. I slowed down to get away from horse _____.

3. Red Cat and I both have coats of paint that are _____.

4. The rule says that every dusty path leads to the

   _____.

5. I am a very smart woman, but none of the things I make

   are _____.

101 SIDE **3**

Name _____

Tubby and the other boats at Dock Three were
sleeping when a very bad storm raced into the bay. The
winds lashed out and rolled the water into large waves.
Soon those waves were crashing against the docks. They
were also crashing against the ships and barges. A
barge longer than three blocks was blown out of place.
That barge was coming right at Dock Three.

1. boy	1. valley
2. point	2. strongest
3. slept	3. robot
4. charge	4. motorboat
5. teacher	5. course

1. school
2. pull
3. heavy
4. against
5. mountain

Rolla Slows Down

One day, Rolla said to herself, "I am number 1, but I am right behind number 8." Rolla thought that she should be far away from number 8. Then it would look as if she was the leader and the other horses were following her.

Rolla said, "I will get far from horse 8." To do that, Rolla slowed down. She went slower and slower. But when she went slower, all the other horses went slower. The music slowed down. The mothers were unhappy. One of them said, "This merry-go-round is so slow, you can't tell if it's going or if it has stopped."

The other horses were not happy with Rolla. Horse 2 kept shouting at Rolla, "Come on, Rolla. Let's get this merry-go-round moving." But Rolla tried as hard as she could to slow down.

At the end of the day, horse 8 was still there, right in front of her. That evening, horse 3 asked, "What are you trying to do?" When Rolla told them, some of the horses started to laugh. Then horse 5 said, "Rolla, would you be happy if you could not see horse 8?"

"Yes," Rolla said. "If I could not see that horse, I would not feel like I was following it. I would feel like the leader."

So the other horses did a lot of talking. When they were done, they smiled and told Rolla they would fix things up.

The next day when Rolla woke up, she looked in front of her and saw mountains and valleys. They were lovely. She couldn't see another horse anywhere in front of her. After a while, she found out that the other horses had made a painting and put it between her and horse 8. But Rolla didn't care. She felt wonderful leading all the horses into the mountains.

So everything is fine now. The horses are happy. The music sounds good. And the mothers and children like the merry-go-round even more than before.

The end.

Side 4

fold first

fold

Name _____

peach •   • It goes on your head.

hat •   • They fit on your feet.

glasses •   • You put it over a shirt.

socks •   • It grows on a tree.

coat •   • They help you to see.

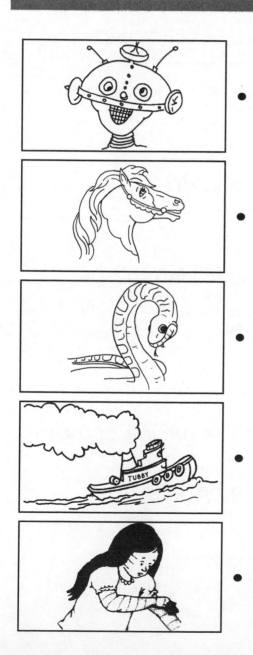

•   • I would love to eat a frog.

•   • I'm much slower, but I'm stronger.

•   • Okay, baby.

•   • But what and when . . .

•   • I hate to see horse 8 in front.

Side 1

1. Who called Molly on the phone?

   _____

   • Bleep   • Mrs. Anderson   • Rolla

2. What did Molly and Mrs. Anderson plan to do today?

   _____

   • make a racing sled   • go swimming   • have lunch

3. Molly didn't talk to Mrs. Anderson on the phone because

   she was _____.

   • in her shop   • out of town   • singing

4. Who talked to Mrs. Anderson on the phone? _____

5. Did Mrs. Anderson know who she was talking to? _____

6. Where did Bleep say they should eat?

   _____

   • at the lake   • at Fifth and Oak   • at First and Elm

7. What did Bleep tell Molly to bring with her?

   _____

   • a book   • a folding chair   • a racing sled

- "Ott and I can train the new genies."

- "I can't take the vow of a genie."

- "Bleep. I never lie."

- "I think Bleep lied to both of us."

- "There is a good place to eat at First and Elm."

- "There is no place to eat at First and Elm."

Are we having fun?

1. Circle the first word.

2. Make a line over the last word.

3. Make three dots under the word after **we.**

4. Box the word **we.**

Side 1

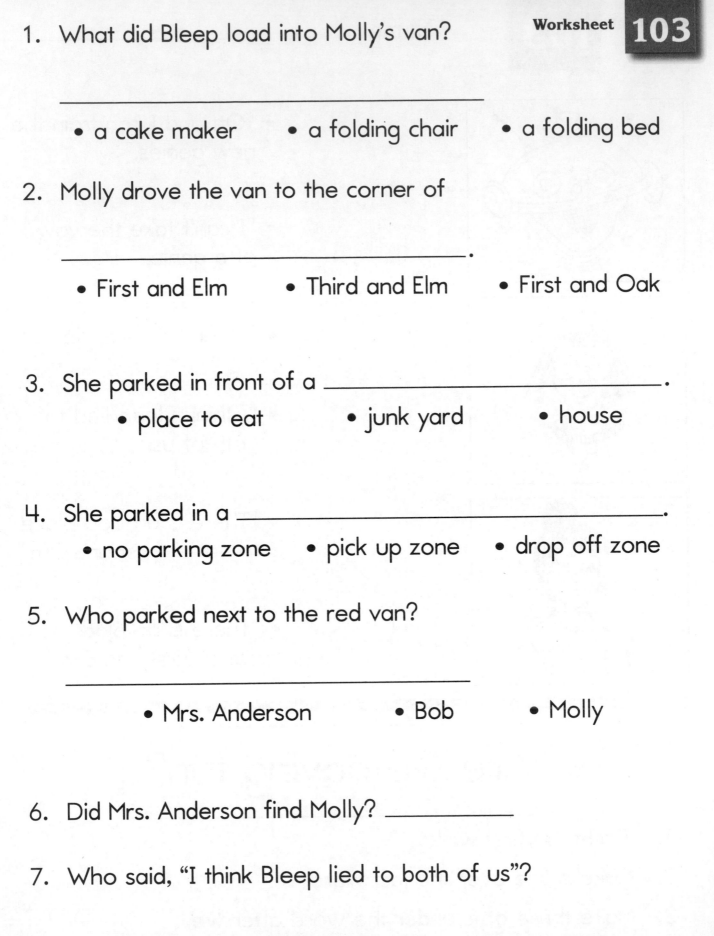

1. What did Bleep load into Molly's van?

_____

• a cake maker   • a folding chair   • a folding bed

2. Molly drove the van to the corner of

_____.

• First and Elm   • Third and Elm   • First and Oak

3. She parked in front of a _____.
   • place to eat   • junk yard   • house

4. She parked in a _____.
   • no parking zone   • pick up zone   • drop off zone

5. Who parked next to the red van?

_____

• Mrs. Anderson   • Bob   • Molly

6. Did Mrs. Anderson find Molly? _____

7. Who said, "I think Bleep lied to both of us"?

_____

Name _____

1. Was Molly right in front of the junk yard when

   Mrs. Anderson found her? _____

2. When they got back to the corner of First and Elm, what

   was missing? _____
   • the car and the van • the racing sled • the cake makers

3. What do the workers do with anything left in the drop off

   zone? _____

4. The worker led Molly and Mrs. Anderson to a great big

   _____.

   • pile of dirt   • pile of parts   • part of a pile

5. Why didn't the workers put the cars back together?

   _____

   • They didn't know how.   • They were tired.
             • They didn't want to.

6. Molly said, "We can get these cars back together by

             "
   _____.

        • noon   • bed time   • dinner time

hat •   • something you sit on

book •   • something you eat

chair •   • something you spend

cash •   • something you put on your
                                 head

egg •   • something you read

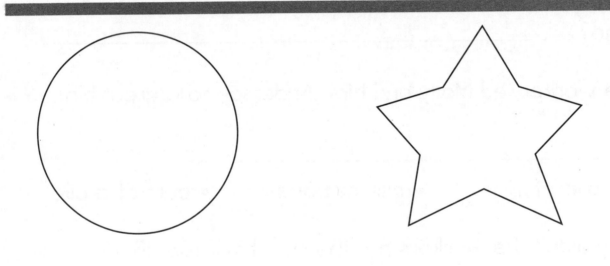

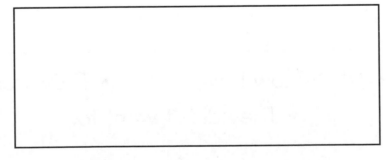

1. Write your first name in the box.
2. Write the word **cat** in the circle.
3. Make a box around the circle.
4. Make a circle in the star.

Name _____

1. Who worked with Molly and Mrs. Anderson at the junk

   yard? _____

        • Bleep   • four workers   • Bob

2. Who cried? _____

3. When Molly got home, she thought the car looked

   _____.

        • red   • sort of pretty   • ugly

4. Molly thought about leaving Bleep at

   _____.

        • a farm   • a no parking zone   • the drop off zone

5. Molly told Bleep that he could not

   _____.

   • say "Bleep" any more   • talk on the phone   • drive a van

6. Who helped put the cars back together the right way?

   _____

   • workers from the junk yard   • workers from a car shop
        • Bob

Side 1

- The fly was next to the cup.

- Something was on the side of a cup.

- The cup was on top of a ball.

- A bird was in the cup.

smile	clocks	mouse	smoke	school

mitten

A.

Name _____

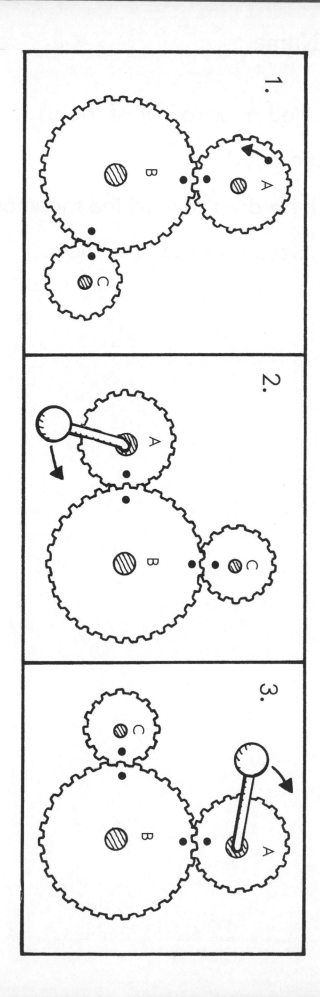

Side 1

Name _____

B.

1. Aunt Martha pulled a turnip out of the dirt.

   The turnip tasted good.

2. The ranger led the dogs toward the mountains.

   The mountains were covered with snow.

Name _____

1. Patty was a mouse that was very _____.

   • old   • small   • large

2. She had _____ brothers.

3. She had _____ sisters.

4. Who else lived with her? _____

5. Patty's voice was very _____.

   • soft   • loud   • tiny

6. What other kind of animal lived in the house with the mice?

   _____

7. Her brothers gave her the name Big Mouse the Big

   _____.

   • Month   • House   • Mouth

1. Write the word **dressing** in the box.
2. Make a line over the **n.**
3. Circle the two letters that come just before **i.**
4. Make a box around the first letter.
5. Make a line below the last three letters.

shop •   • a little store

stones •   • Bikes have two of them.

wheels •   • It's cold and white.

trees •   • They have leaves.

snow •   • small rocks

| bridge | window | mouse | loud | ice |

_____   _____   _____

Side 2

1. One time, Patty shouted when her brothers and sisters

   _____.
   - hid from her   • tickled her   • talked to her

2. How long was it before her brothers could hear well?

   _____
   - six years   • four days   • six days

3. That night, Patty's _____ gave her
   bad news.
   - mother   • brothers   • sisters

4. Who had to stay home? _____

5. Patty's mom and dad smelled _____.
   - new cheese   • new mice   • new cats

6. Who was visiting Arnold? _____
   - Bob   • four cats   • four mice

1. Write the word **somebody** in the box.
2. Circle the first letter.
3. Make a line under the word **some.**
4. Make a line over the last two letters in the box.
5. Make a box around the letter that comes after **d.**

friend •   • shout

party •   • They have feathers.

bedroom •   • a place in a house where you sleep

night •   • You eat, drink, and play games.

yell •   • The sun is not out.

birds •   • a pal

flying   coat   ~~flying~~   (c<u>o</u>in)
                                   4   5
flame   count   flying

        flash   flame   sly
coin
                       coin
float   join
join
        sly
float   trying   frying

Side 2

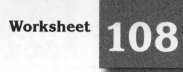

Name _____

1. How many cats were visiting Arnold? _____

2. Did Patty's mom and dad know how many cats were in the

   house? _____

3. Who had to stay behind while the other mice went out?

   _____

4. Was it day time or night time when the mice went out?

   _____

5. The mice were going to the _____.
           • bedroom   • barn   • kitchen

6. How many cats were behind the mice? _____

7. Who was behind those cats? _____

8. How many cats were in front of the family? _____

Three cats played tag.

1. What game did they play? _____

2. Draw a line through the word that tells the game they played.

3. Who played tag? _____

4. Circle the words that tell who played.

5. Write a **v** below the word **played.**

1. Make an **m** on the animal that sq<u>u</u>eaks.

2. Cross out the thing that comes from a bird.

shout •   • the king's wife

lazy •   • heating food

baboon •   • yell

q<u>u</u>een •   • a kind of animal

kids •   • doesn't want to work

cooking •   • boys and girls

Side 2

1. How many cats were behind the mice? _____

2. How many cats were in front of the mice? _____

3. One cat started to leap on Patty's _____.
   - mom   - sister   - brother

4. What did Patty shout? _____

5. What did that cat hit? _____
   - the <u>ce</u>iling   - the wall   - Bob

6. How long did the mice wait before they had a party?

   _____

7. They didn't have a party sooner because

   they _____.
   - couldn't see
   - were sleeping
   - couldn't hear

8. Did Patty have tears of joy or sadness?

   _____

Her old car shook loudly.

1. What shook loudly? _____

2. Circle the three words that tell what shook loudly.

3. What did the car do? _____

4. Make a line over the two words that tell what the car did.

5. Underline the word that has the letters **oo**.

---

whisper •   • brothers, sisters, mother, and father

field •   • jump on something

pounce •   • not a shout

bug •   • not hard

soft •   • an animal with six legs

family •   • a large place where grass grows

Side 2

1. The bragging rats were named

   _____.

   • Gorman and Joan   • Bob and Pam   • Sherlock and Moe

2. What did the rats see on the ground? _____

   • a cat   • an ad   • a boy

3. The ad was for _____.

   • new cars   • Bob   • a circus

4. Who told lies about doing circus tricks?

   _____

5. Who had a plan to make them be quiet?

   _____

   • Bob   • Sherlock and Moe   • the wise old rat

6. The wise old rat said that the rats would have a

   _____.

   • boat   • circus   • race

Side 1

7. Circle the things the rats would do at the circus.
   • ride unicycles   • write a note   • juggle   • cut hair
   • do trapeze tricks   • milk cows   • walk a tight rope

Three girls like eating ice cream.

---

1. What do they like eating? _____

2. Box the words that tell what they like eating.

3. How many girls like eating ice cream? _____

4. Make a star below the word that tells how many girls like eating ice cream.

---

lion •   • listened

window •   • things you read

clouds •   • It's made of glass.

heard •   • an animal that roars

night •   • They are seen in the sky.

books •   • a time when it's dark outside

Side 2

Name _____

One day, Patty the mouse was outside of her house.
Sherlock and Moe were yelling in a field next to that house.
They were fighting about who was the best at diving.
Patty got tired of listening to them, so she shouted, "Be quiet."
Did Sherlock and Moe stop bragging? Patty doesn't know.
Her shout sent the bragging rats flying to the other side of the field.

1. sport
2. shadow
3. whisper
4. afraid
5. tickle

1. mind
2. through
3. circus
4. toward
5. book

1. pounce
2. gray
3. choice
4. joy
5. chew

Tubby the Tug

The fastest motorboats in the bay stayed at Dock Three. But one boat was slow. She was a smoky old tug named Tubby. Tubby was ten times slower than the other boats, but ten times stronger. Tubby's job was to push and pull the biggest ships in and out of the bay.

When Tubby honked her horn and went to work, the other boats got mad. "Stop making all that noise," they would say.

At the end of the day, when Tubby had put the last ship in place, she would go back to Dock Three. Tubby tried to keep quiet, but the other boats would complain. "Get that noisy tug out of here."

One night, a very bad storm raced into the bay. Waves crashed against the ships and barges. One big barge was blown out of place. The other boats woke up and started tugging at their ropes to get free. Tubby was still sleeping. Soon the barge was very close to the dock. The barge made three loud horn blasts.

Those blasts woke Tubby. Tubby thought it was time to work.

"Wow," Tubby said when she saw how close the barge was. "I don't know if I can stop that barge before it smashes everything."

"Oh, please try. Please," the other boats cried.

Tubby went between the barge and the dock. Then she pushed against the barge as hard as she could. Tubby pushed and puffed. The barge started moving slower and slower. Then it stopped. Then it moved slowly back.

"Tubby saved us," the other boats shouted.

But Tubby still had a lot of work. Finally she put that barge in place.

Tubby's motor worked so hard that Tubby stopped. Her motor had blown up.

One of the boats that had been mean to Tubby got free and raced into the bay. He grabbed Tubby's tow rope and pulled her back. That boat had never worked so hard before, but he was glad to do it.

Today, Tubby's motor is fixed. Tubby still honks and puffs smoke and goes to work every morning. But the other boats don't complain. They are proud to have Tubby as their friend.

The end.

Side 4

fold first

fold

Name _____

1. Three ladies picked berries.

   The berries were blue.

2. Our chicken laid an egg.

   The egg was no bigger than a stone.

3. We used a shovel to plant the flower.

   The flower grew all summer long.

Name _____

1. Where was the circus held? _____

   • in a tent   • in a house   • at Bob's place

2. Who was in charge of the circus?

   _____

   • Joan   • the wise old rat   • Gorman

3. What was the first contest? _____

   • riding unicycles   • juggling   • walking the tight rope

4. What was the next contest?

   _____

5. Could the bragging rats ride unicycles? _____

6. Could the bragging rats juggle? _____

7. What did the crowd do when the bragging rats tried to do

   their tricks? _____

   • cried   • slept   • laughed

The yellow dirt was gold.

1. What was the yellow dirt? _____

2. Make a box around the word that tells what the yellow dirt was.

3. Put a **V** below the word **was.**

4. Circle the word that tells what kind of dirt was gold.

1. Make a line over the thing that can b<u>ounc</u>e.

2. Circle the eye.

3. Cross out the thing that is a toy.

4. Box the thing you wear on your foot.

pool •	• a place to swim
burn •	• not slow
bright •	• set something on fire
shout •	• a room in your house for cooking
quick •	• yell
kitchen •	• very light and shiny

Side 2

1. Circle the first contest. Make a line under the last contest.

   - riding unicycles   • riding tigers

   • walking the tight rope   • doing tricks on a trapeze

   • reading books   • juggling   • eating cakes

2. How many bragging rats fell off the trapeze?

   _____

3. What did the crowd do? _____

   • sing   • laugh   • clap

4. Which bragging rat won the juggling contest?

   _____

   • Moe   • Sherlock   • no one

5. What did the crowd think the rats were best at doing?

   _____

   • clowning   • juggling   • riding unicycles

6. Who said, "Here we go again"?

   _____

Side 1

The cat was ready to pounce.

1. Make an **X** over the word **ready.**

2. Who was ready? _____

3. Circle the two words that tell who was ready.

4. What was the cat ready to do? _____

5. Box the word that tells what the cat was ready to do.

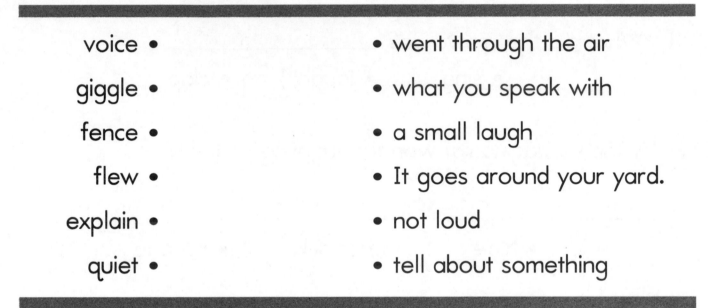

voice •   • went through the air

giggle •   • what you speak with

fence •   • a small laugh

flew •   • It goes around your yard.

explain •   • not loud

quiet •   • tell about something

eyes	rats	people	shadow	mice

_____   _____   _____

Side 2

Name _____

1. What was right between East Town and West Town?

    _____

    • a town   • a farm   • a pond

2. Who lived on the farm? _____

    • Bob   • a robber   • Goober

3. What did Goober play in the evening? _____

    • a violin   • games   • tag

4. Did the people in East Town and West Town like his music?

    _____

5. What didn't the people in these towns like?

    _____

    • Goober's violin   • Goober's pigs   • Goober's truck

6. If the wind was blowing to East Town, most people in that

    town would _____.

    • go to his farm   • go inside   • go for a swim

7. What would some people have on their nose?

_____

• a clothespin   • a ring   • a shoe

| trapeze | violin | Goober | ladder | juggle | clowns |

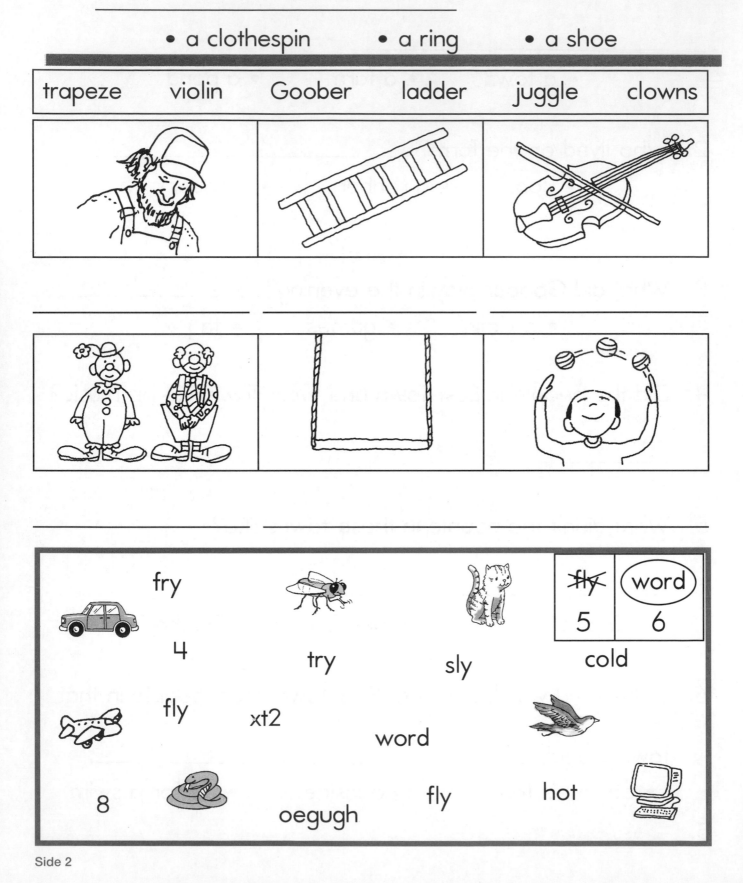

fry

4

fly   xt2

8   oegugh

try   sly   cold

word

fly   hot

~~fly~~	word
5	6

Name _____

- "You bake dice busic."

- "I had my friends over for a pouncing party."

- "My voice is very, very loud."

- "Okay, baby."

- "Goober needs to give his pigs a bath."

- "Everybody laughs when I do my clown tricks."

[box]

1. Write the word **stamp** in the box.
2. Circle the letter that comes after **s**.
3. Make a box around the last letter.
4. Make a line over the letter that comes before **p**.
5. Cross out the **a**.

Side 1

1. Wind blowing east made the smell from Goober's

   farm go to _____.
   - East Town   • West Town   • North Town

2. When the wind was not blowing, who could stay outside?

   _____

   - nobody   • everybody   • only the little girl

3. Did a lot of people go to visit Goober? _____

4. One summer morning, who went to visit Goober?

   _____

   - two men   • his mother   • the little girl

5. What did she take with her?

   - her mother
   - a coat
   _____
   - a package

6. Where did she find Goober?

   - in the house
   - in the barn
   _____
   - in the yard

7. She said, "You bake dice busic." What was she trying to

   say? _____

- "Everyone thinks my pigs really stink."

- "I'll take a package to him every week."

- "I broke my tooth on a turtle shell."

- "What happened to my lovely red sport car?"

- "There is one way to settle this argument."

1. Write the word **snooze** in the box.
2. Circle the letter that does not make a sound.
3. Box the letter before **n.**
4. Cross out the letter after **n.**

1. Who visited Goober? _____

      • his mom   • his dad   • a little girl

2. She told Goober his pigs needed to take a _____.

      • trip   • bath   • pill

3. What did she leave with Goober? _____

      • a package   • a pet   • a pig

4. What was inside? _____

    • bars of pig soap   • soap and clothes   • food and clothes

5. Did Goober give his pigs a bath? _____

6. How did he think they smelled when

    he was done? _____

      • good
      • bad
      • strange

7. Did the girl ever visit Goober again? _____

8. How do Goober's pigs smell now? _____

      • good   • bad   • strange

Name _____

A.

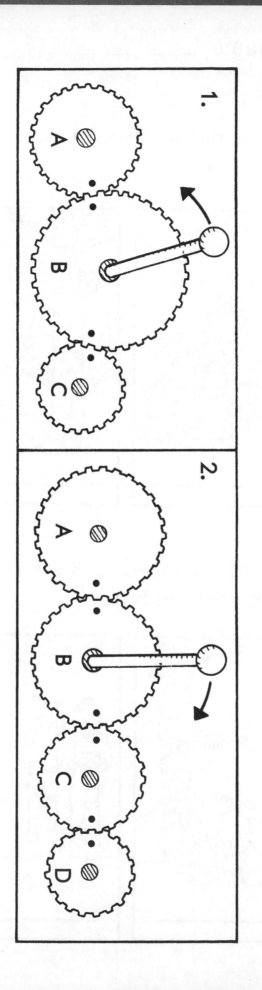

Name _____

B.

1. Three little boys picked strawberries. They were as big as apples.

2. Before the children pulled up the tulips, my sister watered them with the hose.

feet •   • They are all over birds.

hands •   • They are at the end of legs.

feathers •   • They live on farms.

cows •   • They are what you read.

fences •   • They are at the end of arms.

books •   • They go around yards.

snowflake	song

_____ snowball _____

don't

music

doors

mud

doorway

muddy

doors

music

must

music

music

~~doors~~	music
5	6

1. How did Honey get her name?

   _____

   • She was old.   • She was sweet.   • She was yellow.

2. Was Honey mean or nice? _____

3. What was the one thing she did not like?

   • mice
   • cats
   • mean dogs

   _____

4. One of her best pals was a

   • cat
   • pig
   • mouse

   _____.

5. Andrea was very

   • shy
   • big
   • old

   _____.

6. One day a woman came over with

   • a table
   • a robot
   • Sweetie

   _____.

7. Who did Sweetie chase?

   • Andrea
   • the woman
   • Honey

   _____

8. Did that make Honey feel happy? _____

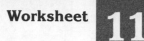

Name _____

- I gave my pigs a bath in a pond.

- I was trapped inside a table cloth.

- I love to make music.

- A little mouse gave me a big bite.

- Someone gave me a package.

| thief | camping | Tubby | unhappy |

foot _____ _____ spider

_____ _____

Side 1

1. Who did Sweetie chase? _____

2. What got stuck on Sweetie's claws?

   _____

   - a table
   - a table cloth
   - a wash cloth

3. What were the only parts of Sweetie that stuck out?

   _____

   - his nose and tail   • his paws   • his ears

4. What did Honey do to teach him a lesson?

   _____

   - bit his nose
   - barked at him
   - bit his tail

5. Where did Honey go after teaching Sweetie a lesson?

   _____

   - in the kitchen   • in the hall   • outside

6. Who did Sweetie think bit him?

   _____

   - Honey
   - Andrea
   - Sweetie

7. Does Sweetie chase mice now? _____

8. Does Sweetie chase birds now? _____

Name _____

1. Dot was Dud's _____.
   - sister   - brother   - mom

2. Were Dot and Dud big dogs or small dogs?

   _____

3. Dot and Dud worked at   - the pet store
                                       - the ranger station
   _____.   - the sea

4. How many other dogs were at the ranger station?

   _____

5. Their job was to find lost   - mountain climbers
                                        - swimmers
   _____.   - goats

6. Who was the best work dog? _____

7. Who would get lost when he went out to find mountain

   climbers? _____

yawn •   • something sweet and sticky

honey •   • something you do before napping

east •   • to wash something by rubbing hard

scrub •   • the other way from north

s<u>ou</u>th •   • not in dan<u>ge</u>r

safe •   • the other way from west

> # The big dog walked home.

1. Who walked home? _____

2. Box the words that tell who walked home.

3. Where did the dog walk? _____

4. Make a line under the word that tells where the big dog walked.

5. How did the big dog get home? _____

6. Write a **v** over the word that tells how the big dog got home.

Name _____

- "I like little birds and little mice."

- "Stop picking on my brother."

- "Don't you think my pigs have a strange smell?"

- "I will try hard. I will. I will."

- "Those red cars are a mess."

- "Not many people come to visit my farm."

- "I met somebody at the corner of First and Elm."

_____

1. Write the word **chair** on the line.
2. Box the two letters that make the first sound.
3. Make a line over the letter that makes the last sound.
4. Make a line under the two letters that make the second sound.
5. Draw what the word tells about.

draw here

1. Did the other dogs believe that Dud would work

   hard? _____

2. When the alarm sounded, it told the dogs that

   _____ was in danger.
   - Dud
   - a climber
   - a ranger

3. The dogs headed _____.
   - north   • south   • west

4. At first, did Dud try to work hard? _____

5. What did he find that was more interesting than sniffing

   snow? _____
   - the climber   • a rabbit   • his shadow

6. He stopped playing with his shadow because the shadow

   _____.
   - chased him   • went away   • turned around

7. Could Dud tell which way was north? _____

8. Which way did he end up going? _____

Name _____

Poor little Andrea was being chased by a mean yellow cat named Sweetie. They had run down the hall and back into the room where Honey was standing. Honey was ready to help Andrea out, but before she could do anything, Andrea and Sweetie darted under the table. Sweetie tried to pounce on Andrea, but his claws got stuck on the table cloth. The table cloth came down over Sweetie like a big white net.

1. great
2. climb
3. wrong
4. lodge
5. flew

1. people
2. argue
3. noisy
4. shadow
5. understand

1. danger
2. middle
3. tight
4. shoe
5. perform

Side 3

Side 4

Patty the Mouse

There once was a very large mouse named Patty. She lived with her mom and dad and her six brothers and nine sisters. All the other mice in her family spoke in a tiny voice. Patty could not speak in a tiny voice. She had a very loud voice.

The mice had to be quiet when they went out. A large gray cat named Arnold lived in the house. If Arnold found the mice while they were sneaking around looking for food, he would pounce on them. One night, Patty's mom and dad told her she could not go out with them because of her loud voice.

Patty's mom and dad were afraid because there were new smells in the house. Arnold had four cats visiting him. They were planning a pouncing party.

From the mouse hole, Patty watched her dad leading the way toward the kitchen. Suddenly, Patty saw three cats following her family into the kitchen.

Patty said to herself, "I must do something to save my family." Patty snuck through the mouse hole, along the edge of the rug, and down the hall. She was now behind the three cats, and the three cats were behind Patty's family.

Patty was going to tell her family, "Cats are behind you. Run." But then she saw two more cats in front of her family. If the mice started to run, they would run right into the cats who were waiting.

One of the cats behind the mice was getting very close to one of Patty's sisters. Patty shouted in her loudest voice, "WATCH OUT."

Patty's voice sent the cats flying. When those cats landed, they were howling and running as fast as they could go.

Three days later, Patty's family gave her a cheese party. Her dad said, "We are very proud of you. You are a brave mouse, and you saved us from those cats. Thank you." After that day Patty went out with her family whenever she wanted.

The end.

fold first

fold

Name _____

bed •   • It lives in water.

fish •   • You drink water from it.

glass •   • People live in it.

broom •   • It's a t<u>oo</u>l for sweeping.

house •   • It's a place for sleeping.

| hard | baby | stink | Dot |

Okay, _____.

Do my pigs really _____?

My sister is named _____.

That mouse can really bite

_____.

1. Dud went past the ranger station and came to the

   _____.

   • north mountains   • south lake   • ski lodge

2. He sniffed to find a _____.

   • kitchen   • fire   • ranger

3. Who let him inside? _____

   • a man   • a woman   • a ranger

4. She gave him soup and _____.

   • bones   • meat scraps   • corn

5. What did Dud do after he ate? _____

   • took a nap   • looked for Dot   • barked

6. Which dog found the lost climber? _____

7. Did the other dogs keep up with Dot? _____

8. Was the climber in good shape? _____

Side 2

Name _____

A.

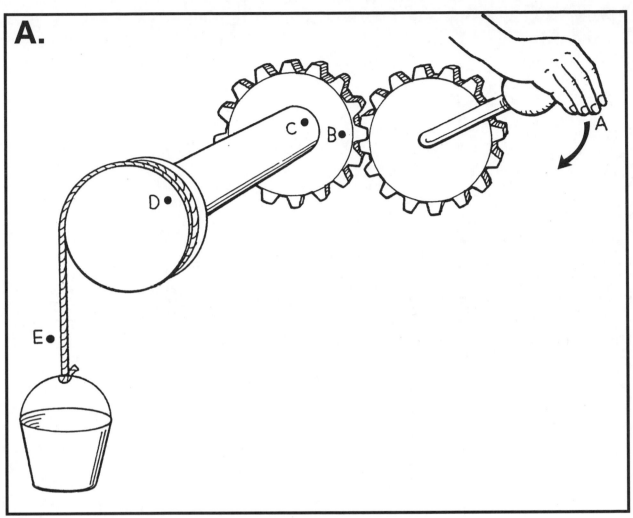

B.

My brothers had dogs. They loved to carry a bone around in their mouth.

Name _____

1. When Dud was sleeping at the lodge, where were the

   other dogs? _____
   • on the mountain   • at the lodge   • at the station

2. Who came to pick Dud up? _____

3. Had the ranger found the lost climber? _____

4. When did the ranger plan to go out again?

   _____

   • that night   • early in the morning   • after noon

5. Did the other dogs complain about Dud getting lost?

   _____

6. When Dud first got into the truck, did he know Dot was

   lost? _____

7. Who stuck up for Dud when he was a puppy?

   _____

| argument | honk | noise | mice | genie |

I am not a very old

_____.

There is one way to settle this

_____.

I love little birds and _____.

When I talk, I make a lot of

_____.

When I go to work, I say honk,

honk, _____.

1. Write the letter **a** in the middle of the line.

2. Write the letter **e** before the letter **a.**

3. Write the letter **r** before the letter **e.**

4. Write the letter **d** after the letter **a.**

5. What word did you write? _____

1. Dud made up his mind to find_____.
   - the ski lodge   • the ranger station   • Dot

2. When the ranger opened the truck door, what did Dud do?

   _____
   - barked   • took a nap   • jumped out

3. Which way did he run? _____

4. Did the other dogs follow him? _____

5. At first, Dud would stop to

   • jump and play

   • snort and sniff

   _____. • bark and howl

6. Then he put his nose in the snow like a snow _____.
   - ball   • plow   • man

7. At last there was a slight smell of _____.
   - ham   • eggs   • Dot

_____ _____

1. Make an **h** on the first line.
2. Make an **n** on the next line.
3. Write an **i** between the **h** and **n**.
4. Write a **k** after the **n**.
5. Make a **t** before the **h**.
6. What word did you write? _____

crawl •	• a place where dogs stay
kennel •	• to move through the air
rabbit •	• move on your hands and knees
cloth •	• a place in the mountains where people stay
lodge •	• an animal with long ears
fly •	• what clothes are made of

tub	shark	scrub	bark

| music | shadow | leaper | doctor | rule |

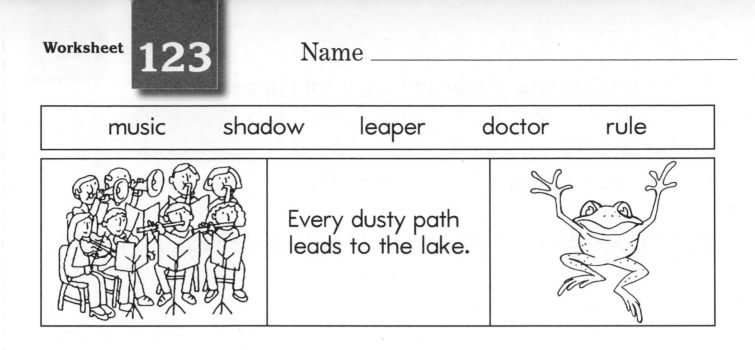

Every dusty path leads to the lake.

_____   _____   _____

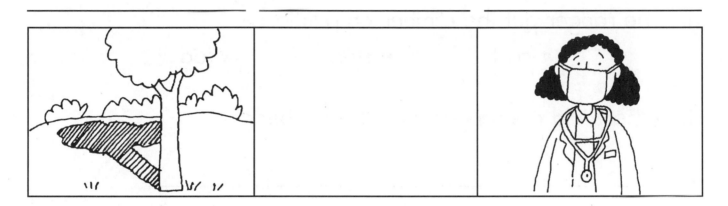

_____   <u>window</u>   _____

broom •   • You do it when you sleep.

dreaming •

math •   • You do it in school.

ladder •

snoring •

read •   • You do work with it.

1. When Dud was closer to Dot, what happened to

   her smell? _____

   • It got stronger.   • It wasn't there.   • It got colder.

2. Did Dot think the climber could make it through the night?

   _____

3. The ranger put the climber on a little _____.

   • cart   • sled   • log

4. Where did the ranger take the climber?

   _____

   • to the ski lodge   • to the mountains   • to the doctor

5. Did the other dogs think Dud was going to be good at his

   job? _____

6. What did the ranger give the dogs to thank them?

   _____

   • a card   • meat scraps and a bone   • soup

7. Who got the ham bone? _____

Name _____

1. What was Bill's last name? _____

2. What was his wife's first name? _____

3. Did Bill do a lot of nice things? _____

4. Did Bill have a problem? _____

5. What was his nickname? _____
   - Bob   - Boring Bull   - Boring Bill

6. When Bill started speaking, what did people do?

   _____
   - slip   - snore   - slurp

7. When Bill asked his wife what he should do, she said,
   " _____ "
   _____.
   - Talk louder   - Sleep more   - Zzzz

8. Bill wanted to be less _____.

Side 1

1. Box the king's wife.
2. Draw a cloud over the house.
3. Put an **X** on the roof of the bus.
4. Draw glasses on the queen's face.

window •   • mean

bridge •   • It's made of glass.

mud •   • not old

new •   • It goes over a stream.

giggle •   • wet dirt

nasty •   • a small laugh

clown   shop   sharp | ~~climb~~ | (sharp) |
                                    | 5 | 4 |

cycle   climb   ship   sheep   close

shape   4   sheep   climb

            sharp   clean   shop

      climb   ship

1. Before the sleep expert came over, Bill was practicing in

   front of _____.

   • his friends   • the mirror   • Milly

2. Bill tried to talk _____.

   • faster and louder   • faster and slower   • louder and slower

3. What else did Bill try to do when he   • smell

   talked? _____   • smear

                                            • smile

4. The sleep expert was from

   _____.

      • the Sleep More Clinic   • the farm   • Bob's place

5. Who put the expert to sleep? _____

6. When did the sleep expert want to come   • tonight

                                                   • never

   back? _____   • tomorrow

7. Who did the expert want to bring with   • patients

                                                  • other experts

   her? _____   • parents

The duck waddled near the pond.

1. What was the duck near? _____

2. Make a line under the two words that tell what the duck was near.

3. Make an **x** below the word **waddled.**

4. Draw a line through the two words that tell who waddled.

---

little •   • a place where grass grows

tiger •   • the day after yesterday

field •   • tiny

today •   • a large cat with stripes

stump •   • a cat's foot

paw •   • what's left after a tree is cut down

I am _____.   _____.

Name _____

A.

| jumped | water | held | | cap |
| swim fins | | nose | wore | pool |

B. When the boys petted the dogs, they wagged their tails.

Name _____

1. How many experts from the Sleep More Clinic visited Bill?

   _____

2. Were all the experts happy about visiting Bill? _____

3. How many experts thought the visit was a waste of time?

   _____

4. The leader told the others to

   _____.

   • ask good questions   • stay awake   • stop eating

5. After Bill talked to the experts for a while, they said,

   " _____ "

   • That was interesting.   • Thank you, Bill.   • Zzzz.

6. Who was the first expert to wake up?

   _____

7. How many experts were still sleeping when the others were

   ready to leave? _____

Side 1

The man behind the horse was old.

1. Underline the two words that tell who was behind the horse.

2. Make an **A** over the last word.

3. Where was the man? _____

4. Box the three words that tell where the man was.

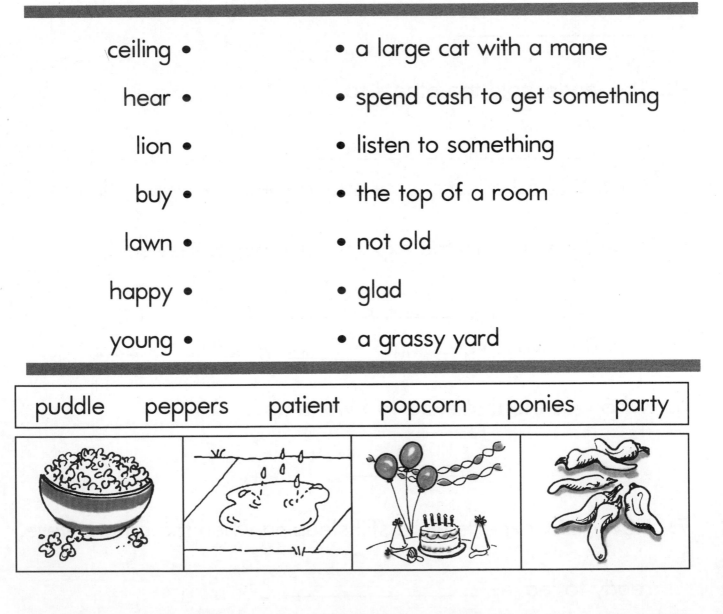

ceiling •   • a large cat with a mane

hear •   • spend cash to get something

lion •   • listen to something

buy •   • the top of a room

lawn •   • not old

happy •   • glad

young •   • a grassy yard

| puddle | peppers | patient | popcorn | ponies | party |

Name _____

1. How did Bill feel after the experts left his place?

   _____

2. Where was Bill at nine-thirty the next morning?

   _____

3. Was Bill able to put the first two patients to sleep?

   _____

4. Then Bill put _____ patients to sleep.
   - five   - twenty   - two

5. How many doctors fell asleep? _____

6. Who was the only one in the room left awake?

   _____

7. Do you think Bill will take the job at the clinic? _____

1. Box the thing that shows minutes and seconds.
2. Draw a hat on the guy.
3. Circle the young person.
4. Make a line under the person who had been a boy.

- "Nobody can help me sleep."

- "I'm just a boring kind of guy."

- "Snort. Zzzz."

- "Would you like to work at our clinic?"

- "Let me tell you something interesting."

Name _____

1. When Bill talked to people in his regular voice, they

   _____ .

2. Did Bill ever find a voice that did not put people to

   sleep? _____

3. Circle the ways that voice was different from his normal
   voice.

   - lower   - slower   - higher
   - louder   - faster   - softer

4. Does Bill use his high voice when he works with patients?

   _____

5. Do people still call him Boring Bill? _____

6. They call him _____ .

Bill asked good questions.

1. Box the two words that tell what he asked.
2. Circle the word that comes after the word **Bill**.

3. Who asked good questions? _____
4. Make a line through the word that tells who asked.

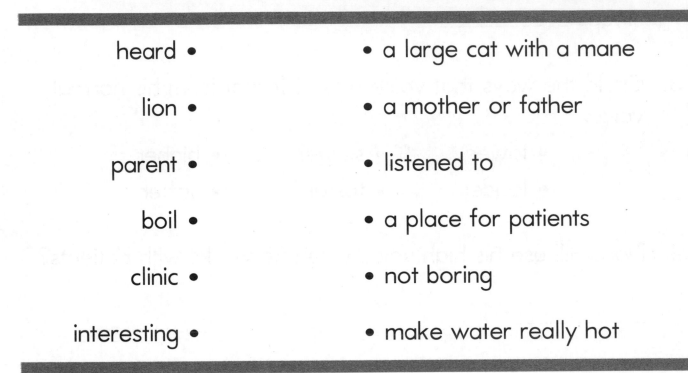

heard •   • a large cat with a mane

lion •   • a mother or father

parent •   • listened to

boil •   • a place for patients

clinic •   • not boring

interesting •   • make water really hot

Name _____

Bill tried to say things that would interest other people. He asked questions and tried to get people to talk about themselves. He tried to say things that were funny. He tried to talk faster and louder. He tried to smile more when he talked. But all those changes made no difference. After Bill was through speaking, everybody else was sleeping. That is why people called him "Boring Bill." That made Bill very sad.

1. station	1. doctor
2. remember	2. tomorrow
3. lady	3. swerve
4. practice	4. except
5. certainly	5. change

1. patient
2. answer
3. amazing
4. regular
5. experts

The Circus

One spring day, the bragging rats saw an ad on the ground for a circus. At once they started to brag.

Sherlock said he was the best at doing circus tricks. Moe said he could do better tricks than Sherlock could ever dream of doing. The rats shouted for a long time. The wise old rat said, "There is only one way to settle this.

We will have a circus. We will see which one of you does the best circus tricks."

So all of the rats worked very hard to set up a circus tent. On the day of the circus, they gathered in the tent.

The first contest was juggling nuts. The bragging rats threw their nuts in the air. Most of them landed on the ground. One landed on Sherlock's head. The crowd roared with laughter.

The wise old rat said, "For the next contest, the rats will ride unicycles."

Both bragging rats tried to ride at the same time. They got on. They ran into each other. They fell down. And they did a lot of yelling at each other. "You knocked me down. Stay out of my way."

The crowd laughed a lot.

After the bragging rats tried to juggle and ride unicycles, they tried walking the tight rope.

Both of the rats quickly fell off the tight rope. The crowd laughed. The last contest was the trapeze.

Both the rats tried to get on the same trapeze, but soon both of them were hanging by one paw. Then they were hanging by no paws. Ouch.

The rats in the crowd laughed so loudly that they could not hear the bragging rats yelling at each other. After the laughter stopped, everybody voted for the rat that did the best circus tricks.

The rat pack didn't think either bragging rat was good at circus tricks. But all of them agreed that the bragging rats were the best clowns anybody had ever seen.

The end.

Side 4

fold first

fold

Name _____

1. Did the two islands in the story look the same? _____

2. Did the people who lived on the two islands look the same?

   _____

3. How tall were the people on Owen's island?

   _____

   • 20 feet   • 1 inch   • 6 feet

4. What did Owen find on the beach? _____
   • a clam   • a bird   • a bottle

5. Had Owen ever seen one of those things before?

   _____

6. The bottle was _____.
   • green   • brown   • red   • yellow

7. Owen's mom told him that some people use bottles to

   send _____.
   • cash   • notes   • fish

- "I'm just a boring kind of guy."

- "I found my sister."

- "I found the climber first."

- "Zzzz."

- "I didn't know north from south."

- "Some people like me to talk in my regular voice."

- "I don't let anyone pick on my brother."

His sister is a dog.

1. What is his sister? _____
2. Circle the word that tells what his sister is.
3. Box the word that comes before **is.**
4. Make a line over the word that starts with the letter **i.**
5. Cross out both words that have three letters.

Side 2

Name _____

early •   • a place where there are teachers

popular •   • not late

school •   • when lots of people like you

clinic •   • It has water all around it.

boring •   • not interesting

island •   • a place where there are doctors

_____

draw here

1. Write **r** on the line.
2. Write **ee** after the **r.**
3. Write **t** before the **r.**
4. Write **s** after the last **e.**
5. Make a drawing of the word you wrote.

arm   clearly   where   burn   sounds
peace   rangers   father   chew   voice

Side 1

1. What did Owen put inside the bottle?
   - a cap
   - a bug
   - a note

   _____

2. How long did the bottle drift in the waves?
   - 3 weeks
   - 3 days
   - 3 hours

   _____

3. At last the bottle came to the island of

   _____.

   - the giants • the little people • the goats

4. Who spotted the bottle? _____
   - Liz • Bob • Dan

5. What were Fizz and Liz throwing in the water?

   _____

   - seeds • snowballs • grains of sand

6. How tall were Fizz and Liz?

   _____

   - less than an inch • more than an inch

7. Did they think the bottle was very big or very small?

   _____

Name _____

A.

1.

2.

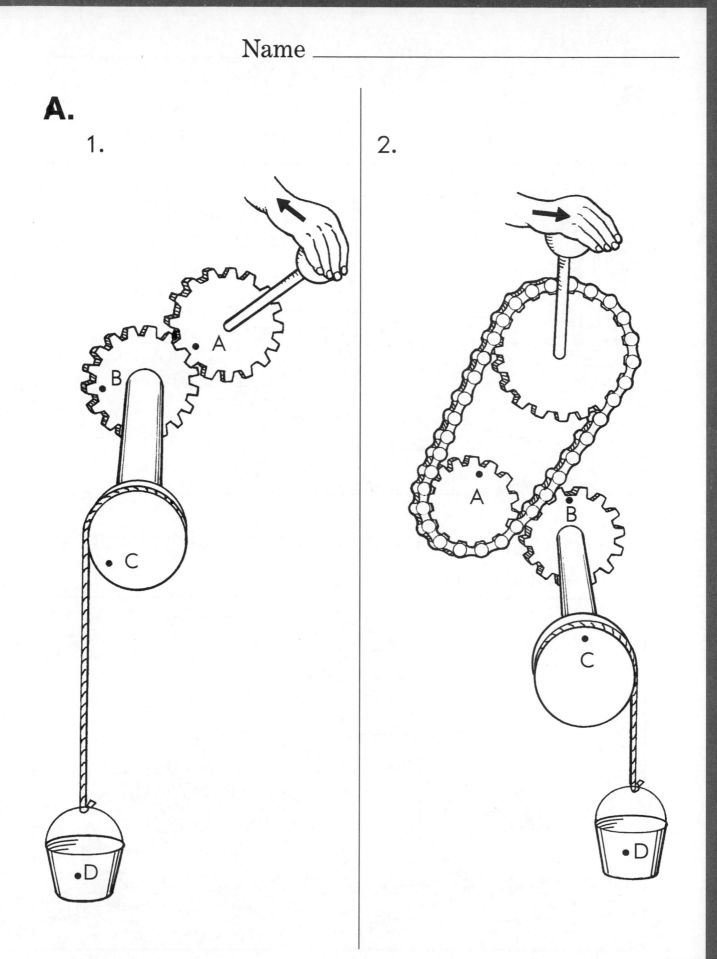

Name _____

B.

1. Our car made a dust cloud. It floated away.

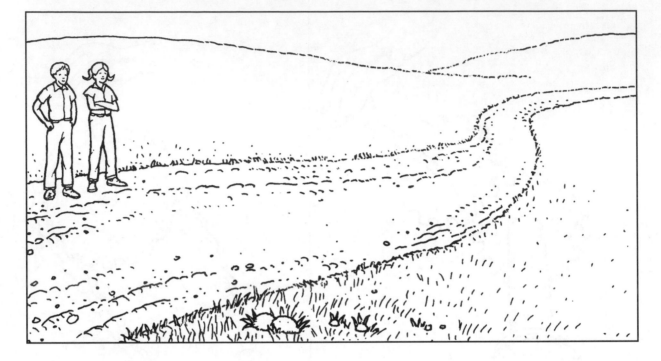

2. A frog was on top of the car. It had big black spots all over.

Name _____

- My mother told me how to send a message.

- I ate soup while the other dogs worked.

- Some spiders are almost as big as I am.

- I can hold a bear like a puppy.

- The other dogs used to get mad at me.

- My racing boat is really a peanut shell.

1. Write the word **always** in the box.
2. Underline the first two letters.
3. Make a box around the last letter.
4. Make a line over the tallest letter.
5. Circle the letter that comes before the letter **y.**
6. Write the letter that comes just before the last letter. _____

Side 1

1. Who found the bottle with Owen's note in it?

   _____

   • Fizz and Liz   • Liz and Bob   • Fizz and Fuzz

2. What did they use for boats? _____

   • sea shells   • peanut shells   • sticks

3. What did they use to push the bottle near the beach?

   _____

   • their boats   • fish   • a ship

4. After they read Owen's note, they thought his island was

   very _____.

   • flat   • old   • strange

5. What was bigger—a bird or Fizz? _____

6. What was bigger—a bird or Owen? _____

7. What did Fizz and Liz write their note with?

   _____

   • burnt paper   • a pencil   • a burnt log

tomorrow •   • something children like to do

play •   • a person who steals things

mittens •   • a person who makes patients feel better

thief •   • something you cook on

stove •   • something you put on your hands

doctor •   • the day after today

<table>
<tr><td>motion</td><td>new</td><td>loudest</td></tr>
<tr><td>nice</td><td>peace</td><td>change</td></tr>
</table>

1. Who found the note from Fizz and Liz?

   _____

2. He showed the note to his _____.
   - pals   - class   - mom and dad

3. Who was the first one who wanted to go to that island?

   _____

   - Owen   - Owen's dad   - Owen's mom

4. At first, who didn't want to go to that island?

   _____

5. After two weeks, did Owen's mom say she would go?

   _____

6. Did they know how long the trip would take? _____

7. How many days did they drift on the sea? _____

8. Where did Owen's dad think they were?

   _____

   - at their island   - at a different island

1. At first, Owen's family thought they were on

    _____.

    • another island   • their island   • a big turtle

2. What did the little people ride like horses?

    _____

        • grasshoppers   • turtles   • horses

3. What did Owen see where his house would be?

    _____

        • another house   • grass   • a tiny barn

4. Where did Fizz and Liz see Owen's name?

    _____

        • on his boat   • in the sand   • on his shirt

5. Everyone went to the beach so they could _____.

                    • eat   • talk   • sleep

6. Circle the things Owen helped the little people make.

        • a ditch   • a waterfall   • a barn   • a car

        • a boat   • a pond   • a park   • a star

shark •   • It's round on all sides.

box •   • It's a big land animal.

circle •   • It's a big bird.

bear •   • It's a big fish.

tent •   • It has corners.

eagle •   • It's something you use when you camp.

beetle   worm   grasshopper   ant   fly   snake   spider   crab

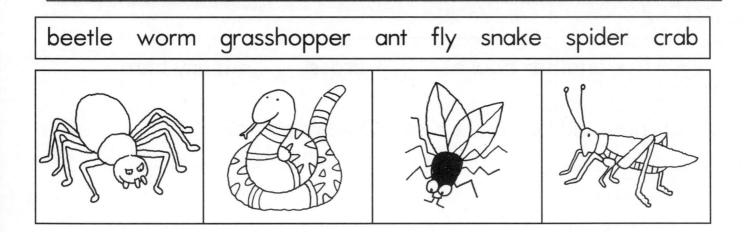

_____   _____   _____   _____

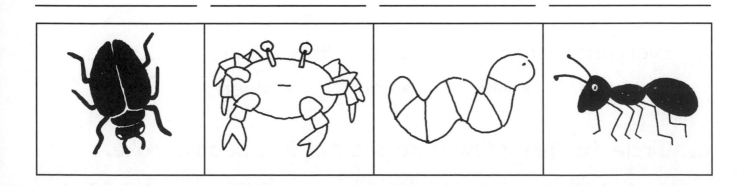

_____   _____   _____   _____

Name _____

Three boys rode bikes.

1. How many **boys rode?** _____

2. Circle the **word that** tells how many.

3. What did **the boys ride?** _____

4. Box the **word that tells** what they rode.

5. Make a line **over all the** words that come before **bikes.**

6. Make a line **under all the** words that come after **boys.**

• • "I put fish in the store house."

• "I can fit between the rocks."

• • "I knew who could get the ring."

• • "I lost my ring."

• "I have my name on my shirt."

• • "They don't call me boring any more."

Side 1

1. How many days did Owen and his family stay with

   the little people? _____

2. Circle all of the things the giants helped do.
   - make a store house
   - dig a cave
   - catch fish
   - make a campground
   - build a mountain
   - bake cakes
   - make a dam
   - dig rows to plant seeds
   - make eight houses

3. Owen's mom lost her _____.

4. Who got the ring? _____

5. What did the giants follow home?

   _____

   - Fizz and Liz
   - a turtle
   - the green bottle

6. What did the giants want the little people to do some

   time? _____

7. Did Fizz and Liz think that they would? _____

1. Who had a plan that would keep the bragging rats quiet?

   _____

   • Patty   • the wise old rat   • Carla and Ott

2. The wise old rat asked which bragging rat was best at

   _____.

3. Which rat said he was the best?

   _____

   • Moe   • Sherlock   • Sherlock and Moe

4. Were the bragging rats good at hiding? _____

5. Did they argue while they were hiding? _____

6. How many hours did the other rats wait before they

   looked for Moe and Sherlock? _____

7. Circle the things the other rats were doing while Moe and
   Sherlock hid.
   • arguing   • reading   • hiding   • whispering
        • running   • enjoying the peace and quiet

ceiling •   • a place where teachers work

newspaper •   • sixty seconds

school •   • the top of a room

young •   • something to read

buy •   • spend cash to get something

minute •   • not old

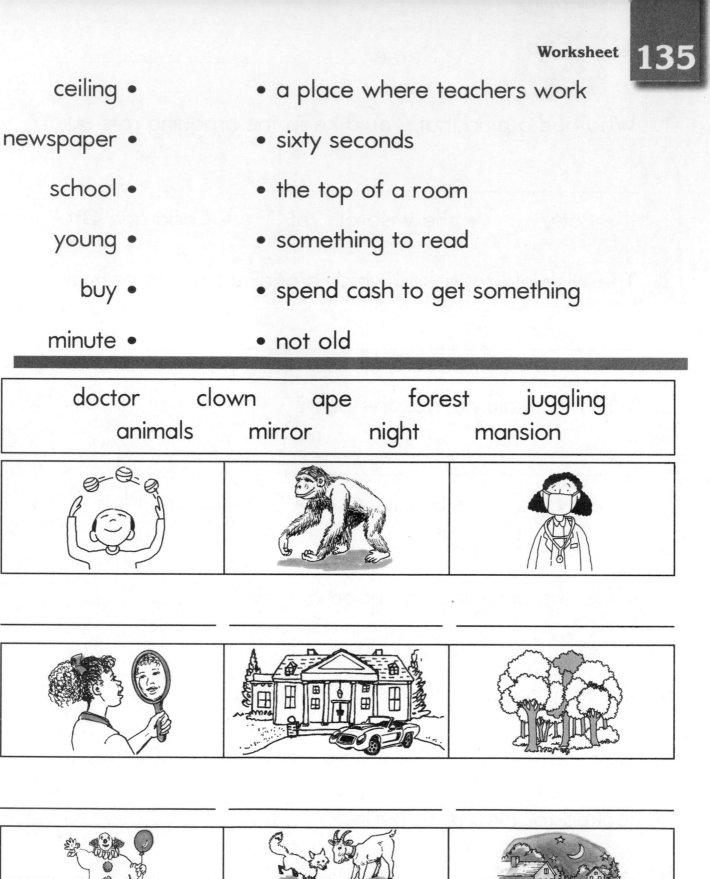

| doctor | clown | ape | forest | juggling |
| animals | mirror | night | mansion |

A.

Name _____

went swimming	stood on a stump
Sherlock	Zelda
painted a picture	Bertha

1.

2.

3.

Side 1

B.

Name _____

1. The girls planted trees. The trees were covered with green leaves.
2. The ladder was next to the house. The house had three windows.
3. Bleep saw Goober. Goober was shaving.

Side 2

1. The bragging rats were _____ to find.

    • hard   • easy

2. On the first day, how long did the pack wait to find the

    bragging rats? _____

    • three days   • three years   • three hours

3. Which bragging rat won the first hiding contest?

    _____

    • Moe   • Sherlock   • neither

4. The next day the pack waited _____ hours
    before they found the bragging rats.

    • four   • eight   • seven

5. Are the hiding contests still going on? _____

6. How does the rest of the pack feel while the bragging rats

    are hiding? _____

see •   • one more time

drop •   • eyes do this

again •   • let something fall

afraid •   • went through the air

flew •   • small

whisper •   • scared

tiny •   • talk quietly

1. Make an **x** through the rooster.

2. Put a **P** on the thing that cooks food.

3. Draw a head coming out of the dress.

4. Circle the thing that belongs in a kitchen.

5. Box the thing with feathers.

Side 2

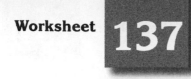

1. Who told Gorman that he needed glasses?

   _____

2. Who made the glasses for Gorman? _____

3. Before Gorman got glasses, could he read the chart from

   ten yards away? _____

4. After Gorman got glasses, how many letters could he

   read? _____

5. When Gorman went to the pond, what fell off?

   _____

6. Who helped Gorman find his glasses?

   _____

7. Who became Gorman's friend?

   _____

glasses	eye	argue	elevator	mansion	street

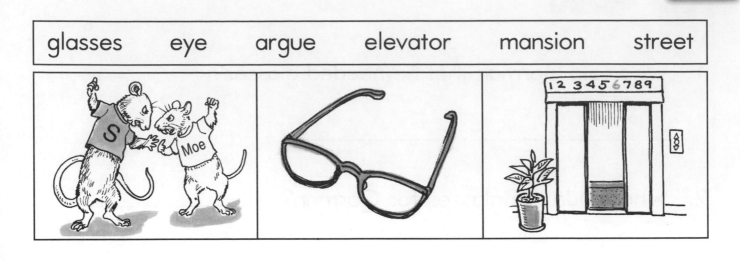

_____   _____   _____

_____   _____   _____

Gorman had new glasses.

1. What did Gorman have? _____
2. Circle the two words that tell what Gorman had.
3. Box the word that comes after **Gorman.**

4. Who had new glasses? _____
5. Cross out the name that tells who had new glasses.

137

Name _____

⭐ Twenty patients came into the room. Bill talked to them for a few minutes, and soon everyone in the room was snoring. Some snoring sounds came from doctors who had been watching Bill work.

Bill was very proud of himself. As he was leaving the clinic, he told some people in the elevator about his new job. He put them to sleep. He almost put the bus driver to sleep, too.

He said to himself, "I must find a new way of talking that isn't boring."

1. enjoy	1. using		1. goodbye
2. hour	2. island		2. message
3. given	3. giant		3. sunlight
4. action	4. beautiful		4. squeaking
5. scratch	5. silence		5. waterfall

Gorman Gets Glasses

Gorman was a goat who did not see well. One day, Gorman came into the barn and ran into a pile of pots. Gorman said, "Pardon me, sir. I didn't see you standing there."

A cow named Clarabelle said, "Gorman, you're speaking to a pot."

Gorman laughed and said, "I was just making a joke."

"No," Clarabelle said. "You need glasses. The vet is coming to the farm today. I'll bet she can make glasses for you."

So that afternoon, the vet gave Gorman an eye test. She set the chart on a tall oak tree. There were letters on the chart. Gorman stood ten yards from the chart. The vet told him, "Read all the letters. Start with the biggest letter at the top of the chart."

Gorman said, "What chart?"

The vet said, "My, my. This goat really needs glasses."

She told Gorman, "I will have glasses for you two weeks from now."

When the vet returned, she put the eye chart in front of the oak tree. She told Gorman to keep his eyes closed as she tied the new glasses around his ears. Then she said, "Open your eyes and tell me what you see."

Gorman looked around and jumped. "Help," he hollered. "What is that great brown and white thing next to me?"

Clarabelle said, "Gorman, that's me."

After Gorman named all the letters on the eye chart, he went to the pond and looked at himself in the water. "Who is that silly looking animal?" he asked.

Just then, his glasses slipped off and fell into the water. Gorman said, "Oh, no. I will never find my glasses now."

A voice said, "Don't say never." That voice came from a big toad. Then the toad said, "Brothers, sisters, and pals, let's see who can find those glasses."

Within seconds, hundreds of toads were in the pond. They found Gorman's glasses, and Gorman was very grateful, of course. After he put on his glasses, he told the leader toad, "You are a strange looking animal, but I would like to be your friend." And that's just what happened.

The end.

fold first

fold

Side 4

Name _____

1. Noser had a very good _____.

2. Who was Noser's best pal? _____

3. Underline some of the things that Noser loved to do.
   - eat paper   • eat cat food   • tip over flower pots
         • stay at home   • sniff things

4. One time Noser found mittens in the yard in

   _____.

   • less than one minute • more than one minute   • an hour

5. Which food did Noser like more, dog food or cat food?

   _____

6. Would Noser get lost if he went far from home?

   _____

7. If Noser was very far from home, what would he use to

   find his way back? _____

Side 1

couch •   • scared

treat •   • something that more than one
                                   person can sit on

afraid •   • something that tastes good

numbers •   • something you wear on
                                   your feet

music •   • one, two, three, four, five . . .

shoes •   • wonderful sounds

Fix up the picture so it matches this description:

    a. There were four dogs in a line.

    b. The first dog had a large collar.

    c. The next dog had large spots.

    d. The third dog had a black tail.

    e. All the dogs wore small hats.

Fix up the picture
so it matches this
description:

a. There were two
   trees.
b. One tree had a
   monkey and a bird
   in it.
c. The other tree had two birds in it.
d. There was a red car near the trees.
e. There was also a red goat near the trees.

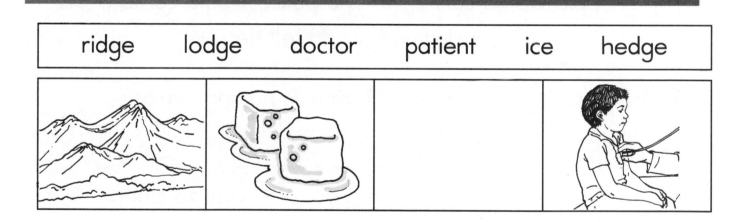

ridge	lodge	doctor	patient	ice	hedge

_____ _____ dress _____

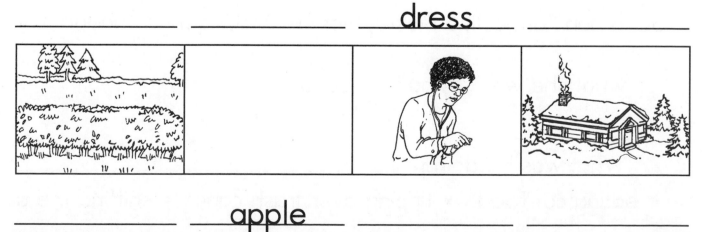

_____ apple _____ _____

1. How often did Noser run away?

   _____

   • once a day   • once a week   • once a month

2. Would he always come home later that day? _____

3. Would he always come home? _____

4. How would Pam find out about the things that Noser did?

   _____

   • People would call.   • The police would come over.
                • Her dad would tell her.

5. What did Noser do when Pam was putting him in

   the yard? _____

   • yawned   • ran away   • went to sleep

6. When Pam called Noser, was he thinking much about

   what she was saying? _____

7. What was he doing? _____
   • eating cat food   • tipping over trash cans   • sniffing the air

1. Did Pam find Noser at night or the next morning?

   _____

2. Where was Noser? _____
   - in the yard   • at school   • in the house

3. Did Noser smell good or bad? _____

4. Where was Noser when Pam got home?

   _____

5. Did he smell good or bad? _____

6. The woman told Pam's mom that Noser chased   • dog
                                                   • cat
   her _____.   • rabbit

7. Where did Fluffy go? _____
   - in a hole   • in a house   • up a tree

The big dog barked at night.

1. When did the big dog bark? _____
2. Circle the words that tell when the big dog barked.

3. What did the big dog do at night? _____
4. Put an **X** over the word that tells what the big dog did at night.

5. What barked at night? _____
6. Box the words that tell what barked at night.

| baboon | mansion | crawl | newspaper | robot | crying |

_____   shoelaces   _____

__rabbit__   _____   _____   _____

Side 2

Name _____

A.

Goober	Paul
painted a pot	fed the pigs
sat on an apple	Fizz and Liz

1.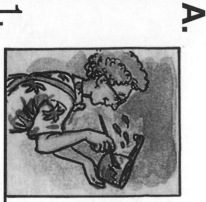

_____

2.

_____

3.

_____

Name _____

B.

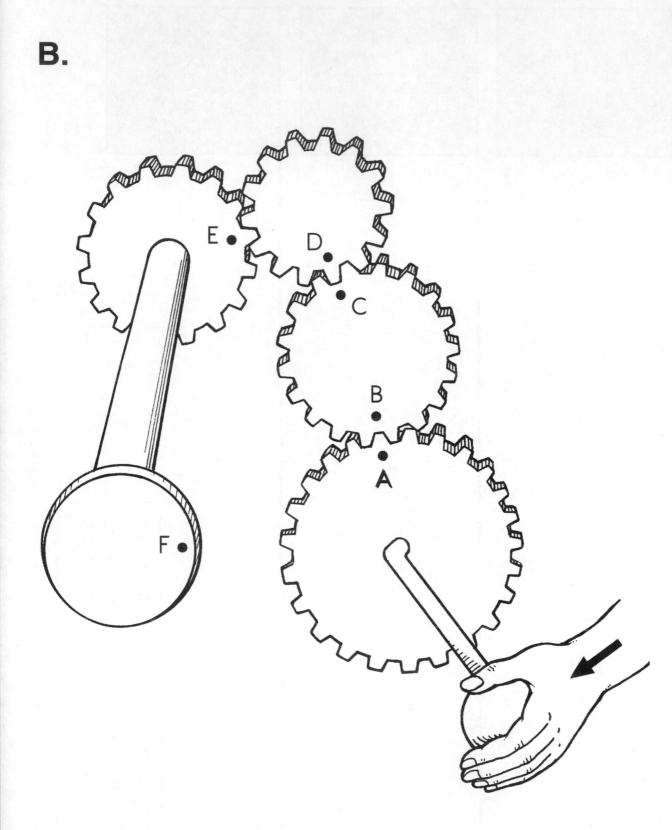

1. Pam's mom told her that Noser would
           • Pam
           • Uncle Dick
   have to live with _____. • Fluffy's owner

2. When Pam went for a walk, there were police cars and

   people near _____.
   • a brown house   • a white house   • a red house

3. Who told Pam what happened there?
           • Bob
           • Uncle Dick
   _____   • a police officer

4. Who was lost? _____
   • a dog   • a baby   • Fluffy

5. The police officer gave Pam the baby's _____.
   • shoe   • rattle   • hat

6. Pam let Noser _____.
   • smell it   • carry it   • hold it

7. Did Noser know what Pam wanted him to do? _____

Fix up the picture so it matches this description:

- The dog sat on a log next to a green frog.

- There was another green frog near the bank of the stream.

- The dog was brown and black.

- Three jumping fish are in the stream.

- The tent was yellow.

collar •	• land with water on all sides
yesterday •	• the shade made by things
gate •	• the day before today
tomorrow •	• something that goes around a dog's neck
island •	• a door in a fence
shadow •	• the day after today

Name _____

1. Pam took Noser and the baby's shoe to

       • the back yard
       • Pam's house
       • the police car

   _____.

2. Where did Pam take Noser after she had him smell the shoe?

   _____

   • through the house   • through a hole   • through the gate

3. Noser led Pam to a house

       • near the corner
       • near a farm
       • near the officer

   _____.

4. Did Noser want to leave the hole? _____

5. What did Pam hear from inside the hole? _____
       • a raccoon   • a cat   • a baby

6. When the hole was bigger, who went

       • Pam
       • Noser
       • a boy

   under the house? _____

7. The police officer said that Noser was a _____.
       • bad dog   • hero   • big dog

Fix up the picture so it matches this description:

- The brown puppy had a ball in its mouth.
- The ball was red and white.
- The black puppy had a bone in its mouth.
- The bone was yellow.
- There were four balls in the box.

| mitten | paint | queen | motorboat | school | sailing |

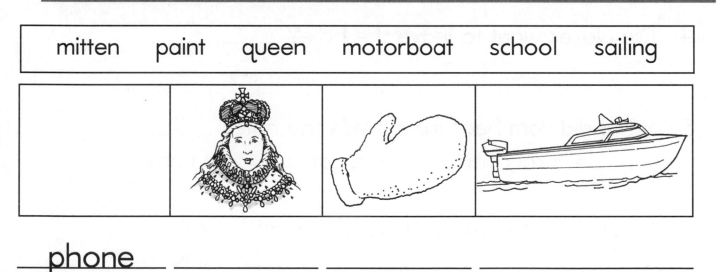

__phone__ _____ _____ _____

_____ _____ _____ __snowflake__

Side 2

At last, Sweetie got free. He looked around the room, but he didn't see Honey. He saw Andrea peeking out of her hole. Sweetie shook his head and said to himself, "That mouse looks really weak, but she can really bite hard."

That was the last time Sweetie chased Andrea. In fact, there are a lot of things that Sweetie does not chase. He doesn't chase mice, and he doesn't even chase little birds.

The end.

fold

Honey and Sweetie

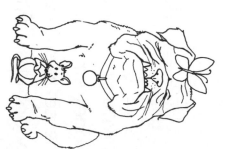

There once was the meanest looking bulldog you ever saw. People were always shocked to find out that this bulldog was named Honey. She got that name because she was as sweet as honey. There was only one thing that Honey didn't like. She really didn't like cats that chased birds, butterflies, or mice. One of Honey's pals was a little gray mouse named Andrea.

under the table. Sweetie tried to pounce on Andrea, but his claws got stuck on the table cloth. He pulled the table cloth off the table, and it fell over him like a big white net. Sweetie was stuck. His yellow tail was sticking out one end, and his nose was sticking out of the other end.

While Sweetie was rolling around and trying to get free, Andrea darted down the hall and into her hole. Honey said to herself, "It is time to teach this cat a lesson." She waddled over to Sweetie and gave his tail a little bite. Then she waddled outside. Sweetie howled.

One day, a woman with a big yellow cat came to Honey's house to visit. The woman and the cat went inside. After a while, Honey got up, yawned, and waddled into the house.

The woman was sitting at the table, but where was the cat? That's what the woman wanted to know, too. She said, "Where did Sweetie go?"

Everybody found out where he was in the next moment. The sounds of running came from the next room. Honey waddled into that room. Sweetie was chasing Andrea, and poor little Andrea was running for her life. They darted

1. What did the newspaper call Noser? _____

2. Who came to Pam's school to tell about Noser?

    _____

    • a police officer   • Pam's mom   • Uncle Dick

3. Was Pam proud of Noser? _____

4. When Pam got home, who was already there?

    _____

    • a police officer   • Uncle Dick   • Pam's dad

5. When did Uncle Dick want Noser to stay with him?

    _____

    • all the time   • on weekends   • on weekdays

6. The people who lived near Pam wanted Noser to

    _____.

    • stay with Pam   • stay at the farm   • go to the pound

7. Underline the days that Noser stays with
   Uncle Dick.

   • Monday • Tuesday • Wednesday
   • Thursday • Friday • Saturday • Sunday

1. Box the animal that lives in the water.

2. Draw a triangle over the tree.

3. Circle the animal that can make things smell bad.

4. Write the name of the animal that has a box

   around it. _____

shovel •   • something you can make music with

counting •   • something you dig holes with

friend •   • someone who knows a lot about something

argument •   • someone who does something wonderful

expert •   • pal

violin •   • a fight using words

hero •   • one, two, three, four . . .

Fix up the picture so it matches this description:

- The first girl in line had black hair.

- She wore a red shirt and blue jeans.

- The last girl in line had red hair.

- Her jeans were black, but they were torn.

- The middle girl in line wore big black boots that went up to her knees.

doorbell •	• Saturday and Sunday
weekend •	• It rings when someone wants to come in your house.
police officer •	• not weak
sure •	• when you are certain
angry •	• between spring and fall
strong •	• when you are mad
summer •	• cop

1. Sweetie went to a house that   • yard

                                     • cat

   had a _____.   • mirror

2. At first, Sweetie just sat in the _____.

          • bedroom   • kitchen   • hall

3. What did he see in another room?   • a table

                                     • a yellow cat

   _____   • a black cat

                                         • Sweetie

4. That cat was really _____.   • black

                                         • shy

5. When Sweetie looked mean, what did the   • looked happy

                                         • ran

   other cat do? _____   • looked mean

6. Sweetie thought the other cat was _____.

          • fast   • old   • small

7. When Sweetie leaped at the cat, what did he hit?

   _____

        • the wall   • the mirror   • the cat

8. Did Sweetie ever find out who that other cat was? _____

Side 2

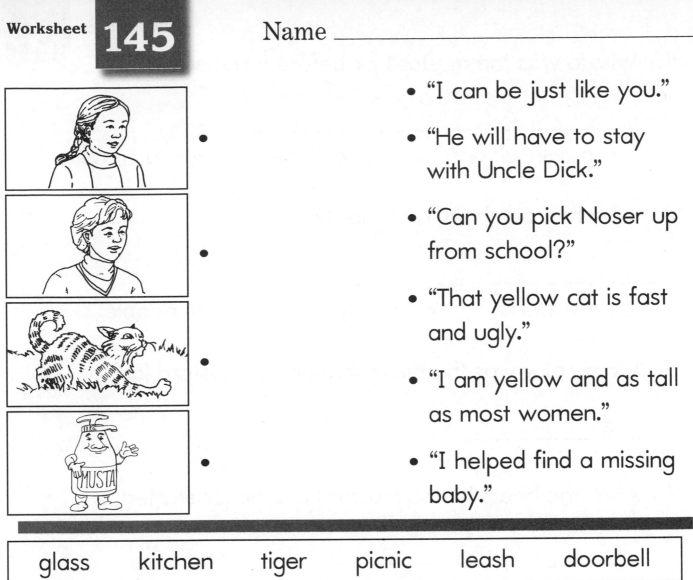

- "I can be just like you."

- "He will have to stay with Uncle Dick."

- "Can you pick Noser up from school?"

- "That yellow cat is fast and ugly."

- "I am yellow and as tall as most women."

- "I helped find a missing baby."

| glass | kitchen | tiger | picnic | leash | doorbell |

_____ shovel   _____ flashlight

_____   _____   _____

1. Where was the mustard jar before it came to life?

   _____

   • in a snack bar   • in a closet   • in a camp

2. Who had a fight in the snack bar?

   _____

   • experts   • cowboys   • space people

3. What color was the beam that hit the mustard jar?

   _____

4. After the beam hit the mustard jar, the jar started to

   _____

   • grow and flow   • spit and sit   • grow and glow

5. Who put out the fires? _____

6. Who did the fire fighters call? _____

7. At the end of this part, the mustard jar was as big

   as _____.

   • a chair   • a woman   • a sack

Name _____

There are 88 squares.

A.

1. Ask another student.

2. Ask your parents.

3. Have a first grader count the squares one time.

4. Have a sixth grader count the squares three times.

B.

1. Tell Sherlock what he said.

2. Tell Sherlock the real number of squares.

3. Tell Sherlock how we found out how many squares there are.

4. Tell Sherlock why we think that number is right.

5. Ask him how he found his number.

1. What did the mustard jar get first? _____
    - legs   - arms   - a mouth

2. What did the mustard jar get next? _____

3. Underline the two words that tell about the mustard jar's legs.
    - stubby   - tall   - fast   - yellow   - skinny   - pink

4. What did the mustard jar do when one of the experts

    laughed? _____
    - squirted water   - squirted mustard   - cried

5. How many experts did the mustard jar squirt? _____

6. Both experts got squirted on their _____.
    - shirt   - pants   - coat

7. What kind of job did the mustard jar want?

    _____
    - police officer   - teacher   - fire fighter

Fix up the picture so it matches this description:

- The man who was wearing glasses had brown hair.
- He also had mustard on his shirt.
- The other man wore a yellow shirt that had short sleeves.
- He wore a black tie.
- His hair was also black.

| quarter | collar | counter | snack | shoes | raccoon |

| _____ | _____ | _____ | _____ |

shovel   haystack

Name _____

Sweetie went into another room and saw something he had never seen before. It was a mirror. That mirror was on a door, and it went all the way to the floor.

Sweetie did not know that it was a mirror. To him, it looked like another part of the room. But as Sweetie moved in front of the mirror, he suddenly saw something that made him very mad. He saw another cat in front of him. He said to himself, "What is that ugly yellow cat in front of me for?"

1. slippery	1. strong
2. empty	2. office
3. during	3. rejoin
4. police	4. disappear
5. press	5. growing

1. jar
2. snack
3. raced
4. squirt
5. burnt

Sweetie and the Mirror

One day the woman who owned Sweetie took him to a friend's house. Sweetie had never been there before. At first, he sat in the kitchen. Then he went into the other rooms. Suddenly he saw something he had never seen before. It was a mirror. That mirror went all the way to the floor.

Sweetie did not know that it was a mirror. To him, it looked like another part of the room. But as Sweetie moved in front of the mirror, he suddenly saw something that made him mad. He saw another cat in front of him. He said

to himself, "What is that ugly yellow cat doing here?"

Then he thought, "I'll show that cat how mean and strong I am." So Sweetie made a mean face. But the other yellow cat made a mean face at the same time Sweetie did. Sweetie showed his teeth, and the other cat did the same thing. Sweetie held up a paw and showed

his long, sharp claws to the other cat. But the other cat showed his claws to Sweetie at the same time. Sweetie said to himself, "That cat may be ugly, but it has to be the fastest cat I have ever seen. As soon as I do something, that cat does it at the same time."

Then Sweetie said, "I know how to scare this cat. I will leap at him." So Sweetie got his legs ready for a big leap, and then he jumped as hard as he could. He went flying through the air. Bonk. He banged his head against the mirror and bounced backward. He landed on his back on the floor. He

rolled around. And finally he looked at the cat in the mirror. That cat was just looking at Sweetie.

Sweetie said to himself, "That cat may be ugly, but that cat is fast, and it can really hit hard."

The next time Sweetie's owner took him to the house with the ugly yellow cat, Sweetie just curled up under the table in the kitchen and stayed there. He never found out who that yellow cat was.

The end.

fold first

fold

1. What kind of job did the mustard jar want?

   _____

2. Underline three things the mustard jar had to wear.

   • helmet   • coat   • rings   • shirt   • cap   • gloves

3. Did any of the clothes in the fire station fit the mustard jar?

   _____

   • wide
   • wet
4. The boots were too _____.   • tall

5. The sleeves on the coat were too _____.

6. Which fire fighter laughed at the mustard jar? _____

7. The fire fighters went to an old _____.

8. Was the mustard jar able to climb the ladder? _____

9. Which fire fighter got stuck in the old store? _____

10. The mustard jar made Sam's leg _____.
    • stiff   • slippery   • cold

Side 1

Fix up the picture so it matches this description:

- The picture showed the girl with her dog and her cat.
- The note on the desk said that she was going to the beach with her friend Donna.
- The pencil on the desk was red.

disjoin •   • to join again

disorder •   • not to join

disappear •   • to take a charge away

discharge •   • to charge again

rejoin •   • to order again

reorder •   • not well ordered

reappear •   • to go away

recharge •   • to appear again

1. What did Sam slip on in the hall? _____

2. He slid on his _____.   • face   • seat   • feet

3. What did he leave behind as he slid along?   • a green beam
                                              • a yellow trail
_____   • a gold ring

4. When Sam was trying to stand up, who ran into him?
                                     • the chief
_____   • the mustard jar
                                     • another fire fighter

5. Sam slid across the street and ran into   • the chief
                                     • the mustard jar
_____.   • the crowd

6. The crowd _____.   • ran
                                     • slid
                                     • laughed

7. What did the mustard jar do when that happened?
                               • laughed
_____ • squirted mustard
                               • talked to Sam

8. How did many people feel about getting squirted?
                               • They didn't mind.
_____ • They liked it.
                               • They didn't like it.

9. The mustard jar went to work as a fire fighter at
                               • Large Stones
_____.   • Big Stone
                               • Hard Stone

Side 1

The brown dog drank water.

1. What drank water? _____

2. Circle the words that tell what drank water.

3. What did the brown dog drink? _____

4. Write an **O** over the word that tells what the brown dog drank.

5. Make a line under the word that tells what the brown dog did.

- "I found a baby under a house."

- "Many people sent me letters complaining about the mustard jar."

- "I can be just like you."

- "That yellow cat is ugly, but very fast."

- "I saved Sam."

- "I fell down when Sam slid into me."

Side 2

Name _____

1. When the mustard jar went to Big Stone,

    it did not bring its _____.
    - helmet
    - gloves
    - coat

2. So it wanted to call _____.
    - the experts
    - the chief
    - the police

3. The mustard jar went into the

    _____.
    - fire station
    - school
    - gas station

4. The clowns were _____ the gas station.
    - robbing   - cleaning   - burning down

5. Who pulled up just after the mustard jar went inside?

    _____

6. How many robbers did the owner think there were?

    _____

7. The police took the mustard jar to the

    _____ station.
    - fire
    - police
    - train

8. Could they take off the mustard jar's outfit? _____

Side 1

Fix up the picture so it matches this description:

- A boy walked toward the front door.

- There was a large window next to the front door.

- There were yellow flowers below that window.

- A cat and bird were on the roof.

gloves •	• the parts of a shirt that cover your arms
sleeves •	• a coin
stubby •	• a snack
quarter •	• things you wear on your feet
empty •	• short and thick
treat •	• not full
boots •	• things to keep your hands warm

Name _____

1. The mustard jar was at the

   _____.

   - fire station
   - police station
   - snack bar

2. It told the police not to push on its _____.

   - lid   - leg   - arm

3. Did the police laugh at the mustard jar? _____

4. How many cops got squirted? _____

5. How many cops got mustard on them? _____

6. They put the mustard jar in a _____.

   - yard
   - cell
   - barn

7. Who else was there? _____

   - the chief   - the experts   - the robbers

8. The robbers thought the mustard jar was

   _____.

   - an expert   - a robber   - a fire fighter

9. Did the robbers laugh at the mustard jar? _____

| glove | mittens | airplane | key | bench | mirror |

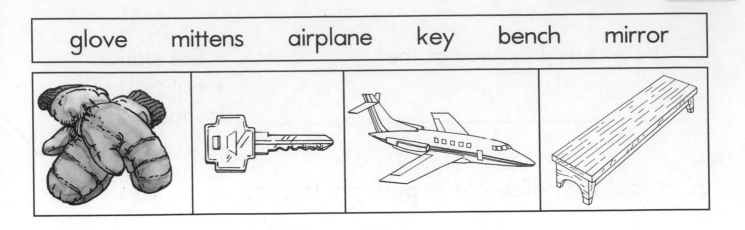

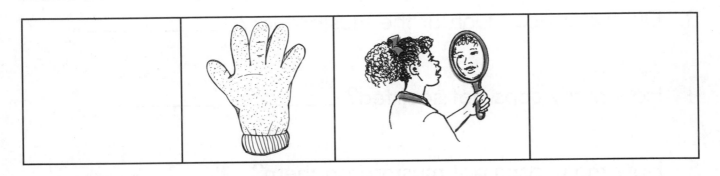

glass _____ _____ hose

Five goats walked on a road.

1. What walked on a road? _____

2. Circle the words that tell what walked on a road.

3. Write **S** above the circled words.

4. Where did five goats walk? _____

5. Make a line over the words that tell where five goats walked.

Worksheet **151**   Name _____

1. At first, who was in the cell with the

   mustard jar? _____
   - the robbers
   - the chief
   - an expert

2. Who came to the cell with a food tray?
   - the mustard jar
   - the robbers
   - a guard

   _____

3. One robber acted _____.
   - happy
   - sick
   - sleeping

4. What did the other robber take from the guard?

   _____   • cards   • keys   • clocks

5. Who said "We're too smart for these guys"?

   _____

6. Who stopped the robbers? _____

7. The first pile of mustard landed
   - in front of
   - on
   - in back of

   _____ the robbers.

8. The next pile landed _____ the robbers.

9. Underline the pile that was bigger.
   - the first pile
   - the second pile
   - the third pile

10. Did the guards thank the mustard jar? _____

Fix up the picture so it matches this description:

- The bus kicked up a big cloud of dust.
- A bike was tied to the roof of the bus.
- The bus was on the driveway going to the house.
- A girl was running from the house toward the bus.

- A robber grabbed my keys.

- Police grabbed my plunger.

- I said, "I'm sick."

- I stopped the robbers.

- A large glop of mustard landed on me.

- I told the other guards who stopped the robbers.

Side 2

Goober

Goober lived on a farm that was right between two towns. When the wind was blowing to the east, most of the people in East Town were not very happy. And when the wind was blowing to the west, most of the people in West Town were not very happy.

Then Goober went down to the pond with the package. He called his pigs. They came running. Then he jumped into the pond with the pigs and scrubbed them until they were pink. Scrub, scrub, scrub. He rubbed and scrubbed and washed and cleaned. When he was done, his pigs were as clean and sweet smelling as anybody in East Town or West Town. He sniffed the air and said, "These pigs really smell strange."

Now things are different in West Town and East Town. People sit outside and listen to Goober's violin music every summer evening. And the air is as sweet as the music they listen to. The little girl from West Town goes to visit Goober every week. She always leaves a package with him, and the people in West Town and East Town are very glad that she does.

The end.

fold

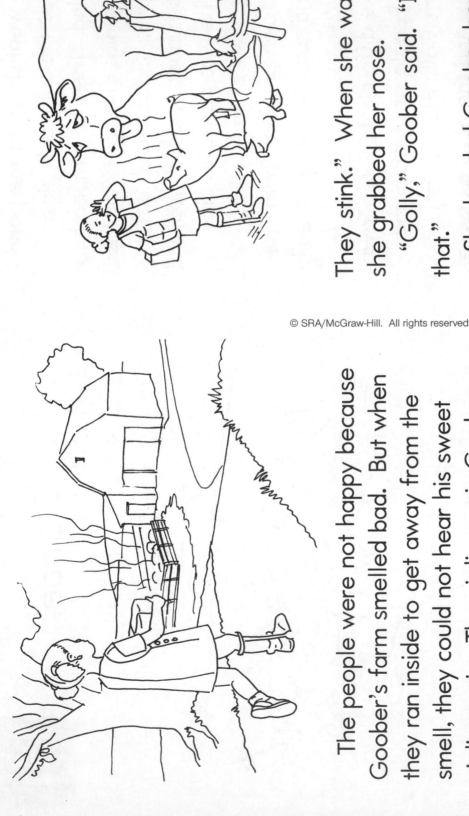

They stink." When she was done talking, she grabbed her nose.

"Golly," Goober said. "I didn't know that."

She handed Goober her package and said, "Here are sub thigs for you." She turned around and ran away.

Goober opened the package. Inside were some bars of pig soap.

The people were not happy because Goober's farm smelled bad. But when they ran inside to get away from the smell, they could not hear his sweet violin music. The violin music Goober played was as sweet as honey.

One day, a little girl went to visit Goober. She had a package with her. She told Goober, "We love your music, but you need to clean up your pigs.

Name _____

1. The jar wanted to be a _____.

    • cop
    • guard
    • chief

2. Did the police chief give the mustard jar a job? _____

3. How many workers were cleaning

    • two
    • three

   up mustard in the hall? _____

    • four

4. The chief took the mustard jar to

    • the station
    • Hillside Farm

   _____.

    • Hillcrest Farm

5. The people who met the mustard jar wanted

    • do a job
    • take a trip

   it to _____.

    • read a book

6. They wanted the mustard jar to make sure

    • take off
    • fly

   that planes didn't _____.

    • land

7. They said that this job might save

    • six people
    • the country

   _____.

    • the world

8. Did the mustard jar take the job? _____

9. Were the people lying to the mustard jar? _____

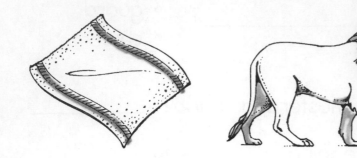

Fix up the picture so it matches this description:

- A brown mouse sniffed some cheese.

- A yellow bar of soap was on the washcloth.

- A blue bird sat on a lion's back.

- A pink flower grew between the lion and the mouse.

disagree •   • to play again

replay •   • to not like

bucket •   • to not agree

jail •   • something in parks to sit on

dollar •   • pail

bench •   • It's worth one hundred cents.

dislike •   • a place with cells and guards

1. The people who were the most upset with the mustard jar

    were the people who _____.
    - sold mustard   • put out fires   • owned stores

2. Circle the other people who were not happy with the
    mustard jar.
    - circus performers   • store owners   • farmers
    - fire fighters   • police officers   • street cleaners
    - snack bar owners

3. The people who were not happy with the mustard jar

    offered it a job at _____.
    - the fire station   • the police station   • Hillside Farm

4. Was the job a real job or a fake job? _____

5. These people wanted to keep the mustard jar from

    _____.
    - putting out fires   • squirting mustard   • getting mad

6. How many days did the mustard jar stay out in the field?

    _____

7. The mustard jar changed itself into what
    - a horse
    - a dog
    kind of animal? _____
    - a rat

Side 1

8. Did the mustard jar look more like a dog or a

mustard jar? _____

| She wore gold slippers on her feet. |

1. What did she wear on her feet?

_____

2. Make a line over the words that tell what she wore on her feet.

3. Who wore the gold slippers? _____

4. Write an **S** over the word that tells who wore the gold slippers.

5. Where did she wear gold slippers? _____

6. Circle the words that tell where she wore gold slippers.

---

fake •	• something you shouldn't talk about
upset •	• not real
toe •	• many people gathered together
burger •	• sad or angry
secret •	• something that is not tame
crowd •	• part of a foot
wild •	• something to eat

Name _____

1. The mustard jar left the field to go to _____.
   • town   • a farm house   • a barn

2. Who walked with the mustard jar? _____

3. Two mean _____ ran out of a farm house.

4. They started to bite _____.
   • the other dog   • the mustard jar   • each other

5. Did the mustard jar stop them? _____

6. What did those dogs have all over them? _____

7. What did the mustard jar come to just   • a park
                                                • a carnival
   outside town? _____   • a circus

8. It was in the _____.
   • police station   • fair grounds   • hallway

9. Did the carnival owner think the mustard jar was funny?

   _____

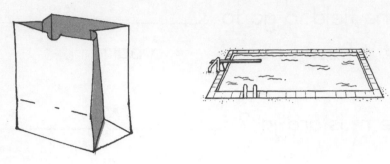

Fix up the picture so it matches this description:
- A boy was getting ready to dive from the diving board.
- He left his towel next to the pool.
- A kite was stuck in the tree.
- An ant was crawling on the sack.

| cell | freezing | juggling | moon | women | elephant |

eye _____ _____ _____ _____

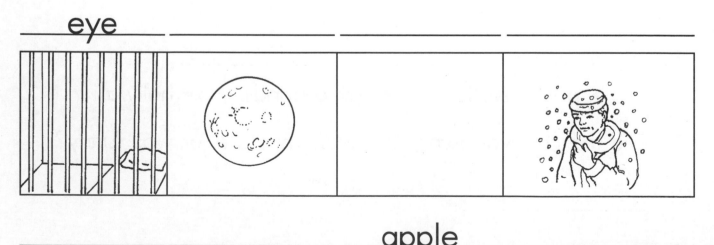

_____ apple _____

1. Who ran the carnival? _____

2. What was the first thing the mustard jar did to make her

   laugh? _____

   • wagged its tail   • howled   • laughed at Hank

3. How many funny things did Hank think the   • five
                                                 • one
   mustard jar could do? _____   • many

4. What did the mustard jar do when Hank was talking?

   _____

   • wagged its tail   • howled   • shot mustard at him

5. How many times did mustard cover Hank? _____

6. How many times was it funny? _____

7. What was the new name Anny made up for the mustard

   jar? _____

8. The mustard jar was going to work for

   _____.

          • the police   • the carnival   • the bank

Fix up the picture so it matches this description:

- A small spotted toad sat on a steer's back.

- The steer sniffed a bush.

- A girl sat in the swing.

- The hawk had black wings.

---

tiny •   • not pretty

stack •   • a place where people work

hidden •   • a pile

city •   • very little

guard •   • a big town

ugly •   • out of sight

office •   • somebody who works in a jail

Side 2

155 SIDE 3

Name _____

⭐ On the third day in the field, the mustard jar got tired of just sitting. The mustard jar thought, "No planes come around here. And I don't have to be in this field to see them." But the mustard jar didn't feel right about leaving the field because it had told the others that it would stay there. Then a dog came by and gave the mustard jar a great idea. "I will become a dog. So I won't leave the field. A dog will leave the field."

A

1. cell
2. glove
3. sign
4. knew
5. sneeze

B

1. couple
2. carry
3. super
4. recharge
5. quarter

C

1. backward
2. enough
3. suppose
4. disagree
5. officer

Boring Bill

Bill Wilson was a nice man, but he was not a very popular person. Bill was boring. He was so boring that every time he started talking, he would put people to sleep.

Bill tried to say things that would interest other people. But it didn't work. After Bill was through speaking, everybody else was sleeping.

One day, Bill got a call from the leader of the Sleep More Clinic. The leader asked Bill to help the Sleep More Clinic with some patients who had not been able to sleep. The next morning, Bill went to the Sleep More Clinic. The leader told Bill that the first patient he would see had not been able to sleep for three nights. Bill talked to that patient a while. In a few minutes, she was sleeping. The same thing happened with the next patient.

After Bill put the second patient to sleep, the leader said, "Why are we working with patients one at a time? Let's bring in all the other patients."

Before Bill went home that day, the leader of the sleep team asked Bill, "Would you like to work at our clinic?"

Bill had a new job. But he still had problems. He was great at putting people to sleep at work, but he still put everybody else to sleep, too.

So Bill kept reading about how to be interesting, and he kept trying different things to be less boring.

At last, he found something that worked. He talked in a high voice and talked faster. Nobody fell asleep.

But Bill's high voice did not work with his patients. So now Bill has two voices. He talks in his regular voice when he is working with patients. But when he is not at work, he speaks in a high voice. That voice sounds a little strange, but it doesn't put people to sleep. Now Bill is pretty popular. And people no longer think he's boring. They call him the Sleep Master.

The end.

fold first

fold

Name _____

1. Wild animals

2. Deep diving

3. Airplanes and rockets

4. Pets

5. Arts and crafts

6. Occupations

7. Sports

8. Collecting things

1. Did the mustard jar know that the job at Hillside Farm

   was a fake? _____

2. The mustard jar took the job with

   the _____.
   - store
   - carnival
   - jail

3. But the mustard jar kept looking at the _____.
   - tent   - sky   - ground

4. At the mustard jar's first act, there was

   _____.
   - a big crowd
   - a small crowd
   - no crowd

5. Did the people like the act? _____

6. The mustard jar was dressed like a

   _____.
   - fire fighter
   - dog
   - cop

   - fire hose
   - shack
   - hot dog

7. The first clown had a _____.

8. The next clown wanted the mustard jar to

   _____.
   - sit on a wire
   - put out a tire
   - put out a fire

9. Did the mustard jar do that? _____

Side 1

Fix up the picture so it matches this description:

- Smoke came from the fireplace in the house.

- A path led from the front door of the house to the forest.

- A deer stood in front of the forest.

- Three sheep were in front of the barn.

enough •	• a kind of circus
glasses •	• the day after yesterday
carnival •	• things you wear to help you see
mustard •	• the day after today
today •	• not too much and not too little
tomorrow •	• the day before today
yesterday •	• something you put on a burger

Side 2

1. A clown took _____ from someone watching the act.

   • a hat
   • money
   • a purse

2. What stopped the clown?

   _____

   • mustard
   • cops
   • clowns

3. Did the clown make an ugly yellow streak along the

   ground? _____

4. The next thing the mustard jar did was to

   change into a _____.

   • pig
   • dog
   • stop sign

5. Did the crowd think the jar was funny? _____

6. Did all the seats get filled? _____

7. After the mustard jar became a dog, the jar became a

   _____.

8. On the next day, it cost _____

   to see the mustard jar's act.

   • more
   • less
   • the same

> # A white fluffy cat ate food.

1. A cat did something with food. What was that?

   _____

2. Write the letter **V** over the word that tells what the cat did with the food.

3. What did the cat eat? _____

4. Circle the word that tells what the cat ate.

5. What ate food? _____

6. Write an **S** under each of the four words that tell what ate food.

elephant	plunger	coins	dollars	baboon	helmet

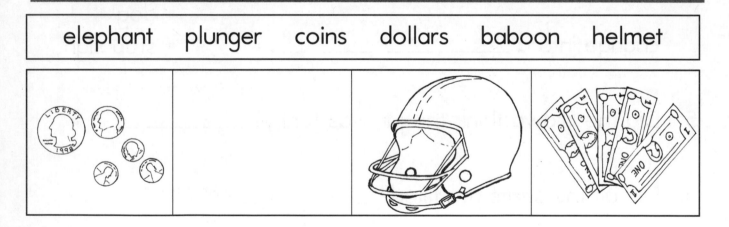

_____ purse _____ _____

___ shack ___ _____ _____

Name _____

1. The chief met with people who
   - made signs
   - sold gas
   - sold mustard

   _____ .

2. They thought the jar had found out about
   - tent
   - trick they played
   - mustard

   the _____ .

3. Did the mustard jar know that the job at Hillside Farm was

   a fake? _____

4. The mustard jar told workers to
   - mustard
   - dogs
   - planes

   look out for _____ .

5. Was the mustard jar's act always the same? _____

6. The fire chief wanted to tell the mustard
   - sorry
   - happy
   - sleepy

   jar that they were _____ .

7. People were really buying
   - more
   - less
   - no

   _____ mustard.

8. Circle three things the mustard jar turned into on the
   second day.
   - bed   • chair   • stop sign   • school   • pig   • dog

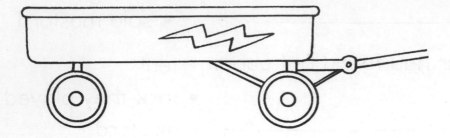

Fix up the picture so it matches this description:

- A dog with black spots pulled the wagon.

- There were two lightning bolts on the side of the wagon.

- Two cats sat in the wagon.

- The wheels of the wagon were red.

change •   • when everything else is taller

enough •   • to make something different

mirror •   • not too much and not too little

empty •   • a large and beautiful house

smooth •   • something you can look at yourself with

mansion •   • not full

shortest •   • not bumpy

Side 2

Name _____

1. In this part, the mustard jar first

   became a _____.
   - stop sign
   - phone
   - goldfish

2. In this part, what was the next thing the mustard jar

   became? _____

3. Who told the mustard jar that the job at Hillside Farm was

   a fake? _____
   - a TV star
   - the fire chief
   - the chief of police

4. The mustard jar told the people who sold mustard to

   _____.
   - think clearly
   - think big
   - think mustard

5. What did the mustard jar leave them

   with? _____
   - mustard
   - gifts
   - hot dogs

6. Who became the greatest star that ever lived?

   _____

Jon and Debby were reading a book.

1. Name the people who were reading a book.

    _____

2. Write **N** over each name of someone who was reading a book.

3. What were Jon and Debby doing with a book?

    _____

4. What were Jon and Debby reading? _____

5. Write **O** over the word that tells what they were reading.

6. Write **A** under the word **reading.**

| tiger | valley | patient | television | telephone | waterfall |

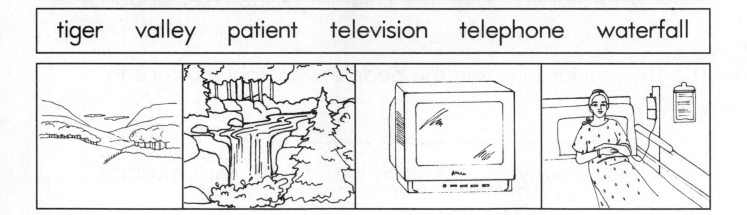

_____ _____ _____ _____

__apple__ __tooth__ _____ _____

Name _____

POPULAR TEXTBOOK STORIES

Number of children:

Who do children want to read about?	1	2	3	4	5	6	7	8	9	10	11	12
Tubby the Tug												
Molly and Bleep												
Patty and the Cats												
The Bragging Rats												
Goober												
Honey and Sweetie												
Dot and Dud												
Boring Bill												
Owen, Fizz, and Liz												
Noser												
The Mustard Jar												

Side 1

Fix up the picture so it matches this description:

- A sock stuck out of a shoe.

- A bug crawled across the toe of the shoe.

- The shoe was next to two balls.

- A tear rolled out of the eye.

---

draw •	• yell and clap
house •	• not sleek
cheer •	• what you find between mountains
dumpy •	• It has walls, doors, roof, and a floor.
telephone •	• make a picture
mountain •	• You use it to talk over long distances.
valley •	• a very large hill

Noser

Noser was a dog that had a great nose. He lived with a family of five people, but his best pal in that family was Pam.

Noser sometimes got into trouble. He would run away and go out sniffing. Pam's mother told Pam that Noser would have to go live somewhere else if he ran away any more. Pam tried to be careful, but Noser kept getting away.

When Pam got home from school, three people who lived near Pam were standing at the door. One of them said, "We have all been here before to tell about the bad things Noser did. We're here this time to tell you that we want Noser to stay around here."

Pam's mom said, "Thank you. But I can't promise that he won't get out."

Pam said, "But if he does, just call me. I'll take care of the mess." Everybody thought that was a good plan.

Noser still lives with Pam. Once in a while, he gets out and goes sniffing, but everybody is proud to have a hero dog live near them.

On Saturdays, Pam goes with Noser to Uncle Dick's farm. She runs through the fields and the woods with Noser, and they have a very good time.

The end.

fold

The police officer led Pam and Noser to the last place the baby was seen. Noser started sniffing. He pulled Pam along to a house near the corner. Noser went to a small hole under the house and sniffed. He scratched at the hole.

Then Pam heard a tiny voice say "Mama."

In minutes the police officer pulled the baby out of the hole. People cheered. The baby's mother cried. She hugged her baby and patted Noser. "Oh, thank you for saving my baby," she said.

The next morning the newspaper had a big story about Noser. It called him a hero. The story said that if Noser hadn't found the baby, the baby could have died.

One day Pam's mom said, "Pam, I called your Uncle Dick and told him about Noser. He said he would let Noser live with him on the farm."

"For how long?" Pam asked.

"Forever," her mom said.

Pam was sad that evening. She took Noser for a walk. She thought it might be her last walk with Noser.

Three blocks from home Pam saw police cars and people in front of a brown house. The baby girl who lived in the house was missing.

Pam thought for a moment and then said to a police officer, "Maybe Noser can find the baby. Noser can find anything."